THE
SAVING HERITAGE

Alfred Awortwe - Adams

authorHOUSE®

AuthorHouse™
1663 Liberty Drive
Bloomington, IN 47403
www.authorhouse.com
Phone: 1 (800) 839-8640

Published by AuthorHouse 02/11/2015

ISBN: 978-1-4969-6993-4 (sc)
ISBN: 978-1-4969-6992-7 (e)

Print information available on the last page.

Any people depicted in stock imagery provided by Thinkstock are models,
and such images are being used for illustrative purposes only.
Certain stock imagery © Thinkstock.

This book is printed on acid-free paper.

Because of the dynamic nature of the Internet, any web addresses or links contained in
this book may have changed since publication and may no longer be valid. The views
expressed in this work are solely those of the author and do not necessarily reflect the
views of the publisher, and the publisher hereby disclaims any responsibility for them.

Scripture quotations marked NKJV are taken from the New King James Version.
Copyright © 1982 by Thomas Nelson, Inc. Used by permission. All rights reserved.

THE SAVING HERITAGE: For those who want to receive the hundredfold and inherit ETERNAL LIFE.

Contents

ACKNOWLEDGEMENT

My deepest gratitude to the Almighty God, the Father of our Lord Jesus Christ, my Lord and my Savior Jesus Christ, and my advocate and Helper The Holy Spirit who through the grace have made this project possible.

I also give my heart fell thanks to the following persons: my daughter Jill Adams and her husband David Seid for their wonderful love towards me and financial support. I extend my appreciation to my sons Michael G. Mensah and Derrick G. Mensah for their strong support in this work. Also my younger daughter Elizabeth Adams for her love. Not left behind, my friend, my church elder and my son Elder William Aduam a strong instrument in this project and the members of Christ Reconciliation Church International of New York.

Twenty percent of the proceed of this book is dedicated to the poor and orphanage around the world and more specially Africa.

INTRODUCTION

The history of the creation in the Holy Bible is the wonders of the hand work of God, known by almost every Christian and even greater amount of unbelievers. It was the lost of the glory which led to the deliverance of the dominion. The dominion is the backbone of man and the extermination of the dominion brought darkness over mankind. While God was searching for someone to retrieve it, man was also looking for ways and means to remove the veil for God to be visible to him to connect a reconciliation, in otherwise a means to return to God.

The bible says in Job 9:24 "The earth is given into the hand of the wicked. He cover the faces of its judges. If it is not he, who else could it be." This quotation in Job is a summary of what happened after creation with man. God loved man more than any other work of his hand but one mistake made by man destroyed every plan God has for man. This led to the advent of Jesus Christ coming down on earth. It was Christ whom the Father sent to the earth to be offered as sacrifice for the remission of the sin committed by man. Christ is the Son of God from Alpha and Omega. He was not deserve to come down to the earth but for being surety of the creation of man, and when God could not find anyone fit for that sacrifice, then Jesus Christ had to come down on earth followed by the Holy Spirit because both were sureties. On the cross Jesus said, It is finished meaning He had retrieved the dominion and had restored it back to its original place which has become The Saving Heritage and has unveil the curtains between God and man and God is now visible to man. Man can now walk to God through Jesus Christ without fear and without restrictions. The Holy Spirit has come down after Christ to protect that appeasement Jesus Christ made on the Cross. For Jesus said I am not leaving you as orphans but will send the helper and comforter who will guide you in all things. Just by accepting Jesus Christ as the Son of God, His death and resurrection, all our sins are forgiven without waiting for forty days and forty nights on the mountains. For the love, that the Father loves us, He has made it so easy for man to return to him, what a saving heritage and this has brought about the accomplishment of this book through His mercy and compassion, THE SAVING HERITAGE.

CHAPTER ONE

PRAYER

MEANING: Prayer is a two way communication with God.. It is a wish hoped for, a desire believed to receive. It is a spiritual communication. Prayer is the only way to communication with God, besides this there is no other way. Prayer is the ceremony in the air, it is one of the highest activities in one's life. It is the basis of one's life. Therefore to refuse to pray to God means to seize to the talk to God. Prayer is a right for human being to communicate with God. There is no other way to reach God. The one offering prayer give unto God and God in turn also give unto the one in prayer. **Prayer superimposes the will of God in one's life because it goes to the root of the problem.** The only way to tire down the works of Satan in one's life. Prayer does not cause faith to work but faith cause prayer to work. Therefore any prayer obstacle is a problem of doubt, doubting the integrity of the word and the ability of God to stand behind his promise in his word [Christ] who lives in us. It is not just prayer that gets result, but it is your spiritual connection with God the father, learning his wisdom, drawing on his strength, being filled with his meekness and spirit in his love that brings result to our prayer.

PURPOSE: We are bound to pray because it sets man apart from all other existence on earth. God made man with eternity of their hearts to pray. Eccl. 3:11 "He has made everything beautiful in its time. Also He has put eternity in their hearts, except that no one can find out the work that God does from beginning to the end." And Jesus said "Blessed are the poor in spirit for theirs is the kingdom of heaven." in otherwise, Jesus is saying "blessed are those who are conscious of their spiritual needs (those who pray) for they will occupy the kingdom of heaven, hence, prayer help us to reach out to the spiritual realm, helping us to live holy and righteous life leading to eternal life, bringing and filling our lives with happiness. We pray whenever we have the need of help from God our Father or we need wisdom or answer to a particular problem that seem beyond human scope or capacity or knowledge. We also pray when we need our heavenly father's comfort, when we are stressed out or when we know we have lost all hope in life, physically and spiritually. We also pray to our Heavenly Father for our mistakes and wrong doings and for forgiveness of our transgressions.

FOCUS: We pray to the father of our Lord Jesus Christ, that was the instruction Jesus gave to us. John 14:13,14 "And whatever you ask in My name, that I will do, that the Father may be glorified in the son. If you ask anything in My name I will do it." By the words of Jesus we have to pray to the father in his name and He will ask the Father to give us what we ask or intercede for us from the Father so that we will glorify the Father for granting our prayers. Praying to the Father means recognizing that He is the creator and above all, and responds to every problem and every situation. Jesus himself set us an example when He was about to be crucified. He came with the disciples to Gethsemane and there He prayed to the Father, "Matt. 26:39 He went a little farther and fell on His face and prayed, O My Father, If it is possible let this cup pass from Me, nevertheless not as I Will but as You Will" Again the second time Matt. 26:42. He went away and prayed, saying "O My Father, if this cup cannot pass away from Me unless I drink it, Your Will be done." Our prayer must also be the will of the Father as Jesus had shown us the example, Let it be your will and not Mine. What is the will of the Father? The will of the Father is asking for something that pleases the Father as to obey and carry out the instruction of the Father, and to contribute to the welfare of humanity and world peace. It is not to ask anything from the Father to go and live high and boasting. This is not the will of the Father. We are also to pray as a church (group), in fellowship or as individual. The change of time has also changed the direction of prayer in these modern times. Elijah, Elisha and the prophets prayed directly to God the Father, without passing through nobody but these days of the New Testament known as the time of grace, unless we believe in Jesus Christ and let Him be our point of contact, our prayer will not reach the Father and will not be granted in John 14:13-15. Jesus also has made it plain to us that prayer could be carried out anywhere, at church service, our study meetings and even on our way to work and in our work place if it's possible. That is the worship in spirit. John 4:20-24 "Our fathers worshiped on this mountain, and you Jews say that in Jerusalem is the place where one ought to worship. "Jesus said to her, "Woman believe Me, the hour is coming when you will neither on this mountain, nor in Jerusalem, worship the Father. You worship what you do not know; we know what we worship, **for salvation is of the Jews.** But the hour is coming and now is when the true worshipers will worship the Father in spirit and in truth; for the Father is seeking such to worship Him. God is spirit, and those who worship Him must worship in spirit and truth."

PRESENTATION: There is so much argument going on among Christians and especially people who are confused about what posture they have to obtain in prayers. Prayer must be conducted in a suitable and comfortable posture. There is no obligation to sit down or to stand upright or to be walking around or fall on your face, whichever is more comfortable must be your posture and not to be under obligation of distress to interrupt your concentration and meditation. Effective prayer is always achieved out of concentration and meditation. Effective prayer must comprise of Exaltation, Worship, Praise, Obedience, Forgive and forget, destruction of the work of the enemies, protection and intersection. As Jesus laid down in Matt.6:9-13

REPEATED MINISTRATION.

In certain cases prayer must be repeated several times before it could yield result, that is known as repeated ministration. Such ministration pertain to deliverance and prayer request, where there is a powerful spirit behind the situation, or a situation God has permitted it, repeated ministration will be necessary:-

Elisha asked Naaman to wash seven times to receive healing. 2Kings 5:10,14.

Elijah prayed seven times before the rain was released 1Kings 18:42-45.

Elijah prayed for a dead boy, he had to stretch himself upon the child three times. 1Kings 17:21-22.

The priests blew the trumpets seven times as they went round the wall seven times at the command of Joshua coupled with the shout and the wall of Jericho fell down flat. Joshua 6:16,20.

Jesus had to minister the second touch before the blind man could see properly. This means until the situation is overcome we must not cease to pray over the situation. Mark 8:22-25.

TWO TYPES OF PRAYER:

1. Defensive Prayer- asking for God's protection and open doors. Matt. 6:9-13, Psalm 30:9-10
2. Offensive Prayer - prayer that will close the doors and put our enemies into trouble and confinement, and destroy their evil plans towards us. Psalm 68:1-2 and Luke 4:35.Psalm 109.

THE FIVE METHODS OF PRAYER:

1. Silence Prayer: Helps us to meditate for God to reveal His mind and direction for whatever plans He has for us and we have. Silence prayer is a gift and not everybody has that gift.
2. Vocal Prayer:- It is helpful to pray aloud sometimes because it stops your mind from wondering from one thing to another. Satan tries every means to take away our prayer life or make our prayer ineffective by means of distracting our concentration and meditation, giving us ungodly thinking and pictures, bringing temptations into our lives, and putting fear into our hearts and bringing discouragement and defeat. Vocal prayer remove stress and take away depression, its a healer.
3. Individual:- where one enters into his closet or a solitary place to have intimacy with God. Mark 1:35.**We do the praying and God our Father does the work. The more people pray the more we engage God our Father into work. God has completed with all the creation, therefore when we do not pray, our Father God have nothing to do. God likes always to engage Himself at work,** that is why He said in Luke 18:1 "men always ought to pray and not lose heart." and also in Thess. 5:17 He said: "pray without ceasing." Also Eph. 6:18 says "praying always with all prayer and supplication in the spirit, being watchful to this end with all perseverance and supplication for all the saints." We engage God

our Father to feed us, cloth us, shelter us, and prosper us. He will have much instruction for the heavenly host.

4. Corporate:- prayer by believers (more than one) in agreement. Jesus said, If two agree on earth concerning anything that they ask, it will be done for them by his Father. Matt. 18:18-20. When one is sick and visits the doctor, the patient believes that the doctor can cure him, and the doctor also believes and trust that he is ordained for that purpose and that through him God will heal the patient, the two do come into agreement in prayer and for that healing will take place in the life of the patient and definitely healing take place. It is not the power in the medicine that heals but the power of the faith agreement. The medicine comes in because we are human and we need a sign and the medicine is just the sign but not the healer. It's just catalyst to their faith. It is the faith in God that heals.

5. Intercessory:- Prayer of intercession can be either corporate or incorporate. It is the most powerful among all the prayer methods, Acts 12:5 Peter was imprisoned to be executed, but the church assembled in a room and prayed day and night for him and an angel rescued him from the jail. Peter learned from Jesus Christ and when Jesus was gone, Peter became the leader, so if he was killed the church would completely collapsed. So the members acted and God also acted, so there was two actions joined to form a great explosion that brought Peter out of Jail. Here, God said YES, and acted immediately. Peter was a good student of Jesus, outspoken and dynamic and learned leadership from Jesus.

GOD'S ANSWER TO Prayer:

The following are the three responses of God to prayer:

1. Wait - God can say it's not time to give you the request but at appropriate time He will do it. It might not help you at that time, which is to your advantage. John 2:3-4.

2. Yes - When God sees the urgency of our request and sees that we need it and it will help us He responds immediately. Luke 7:6. Jesus said yes because it related to human life and based upon

the centurion's faith revealing the deity of Jesus Christ and power of God.

3. No - God can say no when there is danger to the request, when it is for money and fame. Acts 8:18-22. Simon wanted to exchange money for the Holy Spirit for personal fame. Also if you ask for a car but you do not have a driving license, which father will grant such prayer, even we as human as we are. It is a sign of death blinking and a sign of imprisonment.

OUR CONFIDENCE IN GOD TO PRAYER:

1. Nothing is too hard for our God Jer. 32;17; Gen. 18:14.
2. He is faithful and always lives up to His promise. Gen. 12:2-3: Gen. 24:1; 1John 5:13-15
3. He loves us and wants to give us hope and better future. Jer. 29:11=14
4. He has committed Himself to answer our prayers Jer. 33:3; Luke 11:9-10; John 14:11-15
5. Through the Lord's mercies we are not consumed, because His compassion fails not. Lam. 3:22.

`THE EFFECT OF DEFFICIENCY IN PRAYER

1. It is sin not to pray - 1Sam. 12:23 - That is the reason why prayer is a right for the Christian to pray and not a privilege because right cannot be revoke but privilege can be revoke. Without it we will loose God's presence and anointing with us.
2. If we do not pray we deny relationship with God and the spirit of God upon us is quenched and His promise will be broken. 1Thess. 5:17-19, John 14:13-14, James 4:2-3 It is just that sometimes we do not know what to pray for but when we do God works it out for us. Roman 8:26 Likewise the spirit helps in our weaknesses. For we do not know what we should pray for as we ought, but the Spirit Himself makes intercession for us with groaning which cannot be uttered.
3. Prayer must be consistence -we must select specific times for prayer and must be continual. In this way the guide is always present.

THE SIX REASONS TO PRAY.

Prayer makes one turn from his wicked ways and bring the full blessing of God - 2Chr. 7:14.

Prayer enable one to have silence moments with the Lord to reveal Himself. Matt.6:6

Prayer brings love and increases faith in the Lord. - John 15:17, John 14: 13-14; Matt. 21:22

Praying with lifting up holy hands touches the heart of God. - 1Tim. 2:8

Prayer can close and open opportunities. - 1Kings 17:1; 1Kings 18:42-46.

Prayer makes the righteous who do not keep silence not forsaken. - Isaiah 62:6-7; Psalm 37:25

SOME OF THE NAMES OF GOD IN PRAYER.

These are some of the old testament names used in prayer but the new testament says we should pray in the name of Jesus Christ. It is a privilege to use these names in prayer but is not a right to prayer. These names do not answer prayers but make prayer strong. The name of Jesus Christ is a right because is the key for an answer to prayer.

1. El-Roi - Omniscient God [God that sees and knows - Gen. 16:13-14].
2. Elohim saboath - Omnipotent God [God of Host - Jer. 15:16; Psalm 84:8]. The creator. Jam.5:4.
3. Emmanu-El - God with us [Isaiah 7:14]. God made flesh
4. El-Gibor - The mighty Living God [Isaiah 42:13, 9:6].
5. El- Shammah - Omnipresent God [God who is everywhere- Gen. 28:16, Eze. 48:35].
6. El- Jireh - God the Provider [Gen. 22:14].
7. El- Raah - God our Shepherd [Ps. 23:11].
8. El- Rapha - God the Healer [Exo. 15:26].
9. El- Tsidkenu - God our Righteousness [Jer. 33:16].

10. El- Hosenu - God our Maker [Ps. 95:6].
11. El- Shalom - God our Peace [Judges 6:24].
12. Yahweh Zawah- Jehovah Lord the knowledge in the wisdom [Prov. 4:7, 8:12]
13. Yahweh Ethny - Jehovah Lord our Salvation [Ps 68:20, Ps 1:2].
14. El- Dam - God the Merciful.
15. Yahweh Nissi - God the Protector, Our Banner {Exo. 17:15].
16. El-Ethny - God our salvation Ps. 68:20, 62:1-2.
17. El-Shaddai - Almighty God. Gen. 17:1
18. Yahweh - Jehovah Exo. 3:14 I am that I am.
19. Adonai - Master Ps. 69:6, Matt. 23:8
20. El-O'lam - Everlasting God Gen.21:33
21. El-Mekaddeskum - God the sanctifier Exo. 31:13
22. El-Shaphat - The Judge Judges 11:27 23. El-Elyon - Lord the most high God Gen. 14:18

SATANIC INFLUENCE AGAINST PRAYER: (actions:- prayer is rejected or will not honor it.)

God had laid down certain pre-requisites for prayer in our lives. With these, prayer is of no avail. It can become an abomination and God cannot answer it. These are:-

1. Known sin. Isaiah. 59:2-3: Psalm 66:18;
2. Willful disobedience to God's word. Prov. 28:9; Zech. 7:11-13;
3. Selfish motivation. James 4:3; Matt. 6:5
4. Lack of genuine faith. Mark 5:36; James 1:6-8; Hebr. 11:6;
5. Idols in the heart. Jer. 11:9-14; Eze. 8:15-18; 14:1-3;
6. Unforgiving Spirit. Matt. 5:23-24; 6;21-25; Mark 11:25-26;
7. Hypocrisy [self praising, boasting]. 2Chro. 25:19. Matt. 6:5; Prov. 8:15; Mala. 1:6-10; Job 27:8-9;
8. Prideful attitude. Mala. 1:6-10, Job. 27:8-9; Matt.6:5;
9. Refusing home visitation and relationship. 1Peter 2:17;
10. Tithe evasion. Mala. 3:10-12;
11. Refusing charity to the needy. Prov. 21:13, john 3:17-18;
12. Forsaking the Lord and his ways. Jer. 14:10-12;
13. Discouragement. Job. 1:9-10;

14. Evil thoughts. Gen. 37:18-20.

SATANIC INFLUENCE IN PRAYER: (results:- prayer does not even depart)

1. Fear (false, evidence, appearing, rear). 2. spiritual marriage. 3.Stealing (thief). 4. cheating. 5. jealousy. 6. Hatred. 7. Bitterness. 8.Temptation. 9. Defrauding. If a Christian is not praying the right way, then he might have one of these seriously in control of his life, he needs help. Sam. 1 - Hannah was in this position jealousy, hatred, bitterness, fear, cheating, until she change her mind

QUALITIES FOR A SUCCESSFUL PRAYER

1. Faith - total believe in CHRIST.
2. Broken Hearted - total repentance. Discarding bitterness and forgiving others.
3. Righteousness - ask for forgiveness of sin and be someone whose sins are forgiven. God fearing and someone charitable and does not jumps into conclusion.
4. Worship - One with humility, a peace maker.

God gives the prayerful believer the Holy Spirit's timely Prophetic gifts eg. Dreams and vision, which are available to all believers. Acts 2:17. A believer's life begins with prayer and grows in prayer, which is the privilege of coming to God's throne in faith.

THE HOLY GHOST ANALOGY

Without the Holy Ghost, our prayer will be occupied by Satan who will give us his own spirit and prevent us from praying to our Heavenly Father.

To receive the Holy Ghost is like the car battery. A new car battery needs a twelve-hour charging and afterwards it must be continually charged by the alternator, if you have to operate the electrical appliances of the car. Without continually charging the battery, the battery will discharge and there will be no power in that battery to carry out or operate the equipments.

This electro-analogy is being compared to the Holy Ghost. You need a long positive continuous prayers to pull the Holy Ghost into your life. To be fully charged with the Holy Ghost, you need long continuous prayer and fasting or probably with a man of God laying hands on you for the impartation in prayer, and is the fastest way. Acts 8:17, is like using the highway emergency equipment to give a discharged battery a jump. Little short continuous prayers are good but does not bring down the Holy Ghost - it does not fully charge your spirit with the Holy Ghost. After pulling the Holy Ghost in your life you need to be charging it with daily prayer. Once you continue to carry out daily life your spiritual battery continue to discharge, therefore you need to continually charge it, otherwise you might loose the anointing of the Holy Ghost - that is upon you. To be properly and fully anointed: prayer, fasting, charity, meekness, love, righteousness are the essentials of the Holy Ghost. Many people say long hours prayer is not necessary, Even The Lord Jesus himself whom we follow, God the Son, prayed for long hours; Luke 6:12. "And it came to pass in those days that he went out into a mountain to pray, and continued all night in prayer to God." Long hours of prayer remove wickedness, lust, sin generally and weakness. Those who are committed to sin and unrighteousness, have little or no prayer in them. When you see such habit, you should involve yourself in positive long hours of prayers, to subdue the works of Satan. Such habits are not of God and those who think they are spiritual and involve in such habitual life must know that they are putting the seed of Satan into the seed of God as is written in: Matthew 13:24-30 "The kingdom of Heaven is like a man who sowed good see in his field. But while everyone was sleeping, his enemies came and sowed weeds among the wheat, and went away. When the wheat sprouted and formed heads, then the weeds also appeared. The owner's servants came to him and said, Sir, didn't you sowed good seed in your field? Where then did the weeds come from? He said an enemy has done this. The servants said to him, Do you want us then to go and gather them up. But he said, No, lest while you gather up the tares you also uproot the wheat with them. Let both grow together until harvest, and at the time of the harvest I will say to the reapers, First gather together the tares and bind them in bundles to burn them, but gather the wheat into my barn."

If we don't stop the unclean behavior now, there will be a time we have to wait for it to grow together with the righteous behavior in us, then we can identify and cut them out to destroy them. Waiting for them to grow together to identify them, can take fifty years, hundred years or more, we may die in our sins, and that will be a hindrance to enter into Christ kingdom. We have to do something about it now and now is the hour. If the Son forgives our sins we will be truly forgiven, commit all our cares unto Our Lord and Savior Jesus Christ and embrace Him totally and we will truly be free men unto eternity.

QUIZ

1. What is prayer?

Prayer is a wish hoped for and a way to communicate with God.

2. Is prayer a privilege or right?

It is a right, that's why God has committed Himself to answer your prayer and has no choice to deny your prayer except that it may endanger the one's life. It's like the citizenship, it is a right to everyone born in that country and could not be revoked. If prayer does not based on the will of God, that prayer right will diminished with time.

3. What are the two kinds of prayer in use?
   (a) Defensive prayer (b) Offensive Prayer

4. Give the five method of prayer.
   (a) Silence (b) Vocal Prayer (c) intercessory (d) corporate (e) individual.

5. Why do we have to pray in Jesus name?

Because Jesus is the point of contact for our prayers. (a) John 14:6 I am the way, the truth and the life. No one can come to the father unless by me. (b) John 6: 29 This is the work of God that you believe in Him whom He sent.

6. What give us confidence that our prayer to God will be answered if we based on His will?
   (a) Nothing is too hard for our God. Jer. 32:17
   (b) He is faithful and always lives up to His promise. 1John 5:13-15
   (c) He loves us and wants to give us hope and better future. Jer 29:11-14
   (d) by His mercies we are not consumed. Lam. 3:22.
   (e) He has committed Himself to answer our prayers. Jer 33:3, Luke 11:9-10, John 14:11-15.

7. What are the qualities for a successful prayer? Or What does one have to do for his or her prayer to be answered?
   (a) Have faith - (total believe in God with your mind, your heart and substance.)
   (b) Have the spirit of worship psalm 95:6-7 spirit of humility that's humbleness and obedience
   (c) Be righteous – able to confess and ask for forgiveness of sin – some one whose sins are forgiven Isaiah 43:25 and full of good works Acts 9:36.
   (d) Broken Hearted be able to discard bitterness and forgive others. Heb. 12:14-15

8. What is God's response to prayer-?
   (a) Yes - Luke 7:6 (b) No - Acts 8:18-22 (c) Wait - John 2:3-4

MARRIAGE

MEMORY VERSE: Gen. 2:18, 24. And the Lord God said," it is not good that the man should be alone; I will make him an help meet for him. Therefore shall a man leave his father and his mother and shall cleave unto his wife and they shall be one flesh".

DEFINITION OF MARRIAGE:- Marriage is a concept where by two opposite sex are united whose unification is ordained by God and approved by the native constitution. This unification is unto procreation and trusting one another in love.

1Cor. 7:39. The wife is bound by the law as long as her husband liveth; but if the husband be dead she is at liberty to be married to whom she will; only in the Lord.

INSTITUTION OF MARRIAGE:-Marriage was originally instituted by God. God Himself saw that it was not good for man to be alone so He made a helper for the man. She is not a servant or slave, but a helper. Beating a woman means beating yourself, for she is the rib (part) of a man. Genesis 2:18, 21-24. "And the Lord God said, It is not good that the man should be alone; I will make him an help meet for him. And the Lord God caused a deep sleep to fall upon Adam, and he slept: and He took one of his ribs and He closed up the flesh instead thereof; And the rib which the Lord God had taken from the man, made he a woman, and brought her unto the man. And Adam said this is the bone of my bone and the flesh of my flesh: she shall be called woman, because she was taken out of man: Therefore shall a man leave his father and mother, and shall cleave unto his wife: and they shall be one flesh." (Mark 10:6-8), "And He answered and said unto them, Have ye not read that He which made them at the beginning made them male and female. And said, for this cause shall a man leave father and mother and shall cleave to his wife and they twain shall be one flesh. Wherefore they are no more twain, but one flesh. What therefore God hath joined together, let no man put asunder."

PURPOSE OF MARRIAGE: For the woman to be the helper to the man, Genesis 2:18 and to produce their kind (to multiply) and be fruitful, Genesis 1:28; and for the man to provide for the wife with all her needs. Originally woman take care of the household, put the house in order, take care of the children in the house. The man is to work and bring food, clothing and provide accommodation for the family. Genesis 3:17-19 'And unto Adam He said, because thou has hearkened unto the voice of thy wife and has eaten of the tree of which I commended thee, saying thou shall not eat of it: curse is the ground for thy sake: In sorrow shall thou eat of it all the days of thy life. Thorns **(illness and sickness)** also and thistle **(the struggle and difficulties in life)** shall it bring forth to thee: and thou shall eat the herb of the field; In the sweat of thy face shall thou eat bread, till thou return unto the ground: for out of it was thou taken, for dust thou art and unto dust shall thou return. The Lord gave work to man and child bearing to woman'.

FUNCTION OF MARRIAGE:- To cleave unto one another, binding themselves to each other, respecting the marriage bed or keeping the marriage bed undefiled, no cheating on one another. Respect your position in the marriage eg. the man as the head of the family, 1Cor. 11:3 "But I will have you know that the head of every man is Christ; and the head of the woman is the man; and the head of Christ is God". 1Peter 3:5-7; "For after this manner in the old time the holy women also who trusted in God, adorned themselves, being in subjection unto their own husbands. Even as Sarah obeyed Abraham, calling him lord: whose daughter ye are, as long as ye do well and are not afraid, with any amazement. Likewise ye husbands, dwell with them according to knowledge, giving honor unto the wife, as unto the weaker vessels, and as being heirs together of the grace of life; that your prayer be not hindered". The wife administers the house, in otherwise the administrator of the house. Marriage will not function when the two are not bound together and they do not know their position in the marriage. As it is said in Matt. 19:5-6. "And said, For this cause shall a man leave father and mother and shall cleave to his wife and they twain shall be one flesh. Wherefore they are no more twain but one flesh. What therefore God hath join together let not man put asunder". 1Cor. 7:10-11. "And unto the married I command, yet not I, but the Lord, let not the wife depart from her husband. But even if she depart, let her remain unmarried or be reconciled to her husband: and let not the husband put away his wife". 1Cor. 7:27. "Art thou bound unto a wife, seek not to be loosed; Art thou loosed from a wife, seek not a wife". Rom. 7:2-3 "For the woman which hath a husband is bound by the law to her husband so long as he liveth, but if the husband be dead she is loosed from the law of her husband". **(Q: what if the wife should kill the husband and marry another?) that will be terrible evil and unacceptable, Num. 35:33. when you kill you pollute, and bring curse upon the land and the only way to clean up the mess is by the blood of the murderer.)** Rom. 7:3. "So then if while her husband lives she be married to another man, she shall be called an adulteress, but if her husband be dead, she is free from that law; so that she is no adulteress though she be married to another man". Matt. 5:32. "But I say unto you, That whosoever shall put away his wife, saving for the cause of fornication, causeth her to commit adultery; and whosoever shall marry her that is divorced committed adultery." Luke 16:18. "Whosoever, put away his wife, and marry another commit adultery: and whosoever marries her that is put away from her husband commits adultery." It is the will of God that every man gets his wife and every woman also gets her husband, therefore divorce is not the will of God and Jesus made it point blank. It is a straight forward saying.

THE JOY OF MARRIAGE:-

1. Husbands must love their wives and wives must also respect and honor or reverend their husbands Beating your wife means beating yourself because she is the rib (part) of the man. The wife is not a servant or slave, but a helper. Being weaker vessel does not make one a servant. She takes all the administrative responsibilities in the house. The wife is not designed to compete with the husband but these modern days the situation has changed, all are going out there to struggle. That was not the plan of God. Eph. 5:28-31. "So husband ought to love their wives as their own bodies; he who loves his wife loves himself. For no one ever hated his own flesh, but nourishes and cherishes it, just as the Lord does the church. For we are members of his body, of His flesh and of His bones. For

this reason a man shall leave his father and mother and be join to his wife and the two shall become one flesh."

2. Do not compare your past relationship with the present, either by the husband nor the wife. Do not let such words be heard from your mouth. Focus ahead and not turn back;. 1Cor. 9:24-26. Apostle Paul is saying those who run proceed onward, if we want the price. Therefore if we want our marriages to succeed then we should only focus ahead and forget the past.

3. Stop any negative comments about yourselves (wife and husband) comparing husband or wife to friends and condemning your own marriage which is very precious in life. Apostle Paul is saying corrupt communication concerning our marriage will physically and spiritually damage our marriage but speak that which will put life into our marriages. We should also do away with every bitterness so that it will not aggravate the Holy Spirit who is our helper to hinder answer to our prayers, Rom. 6:12-16.

4. The wife is not a servant or slave but a helper. Some teachers portray marriage and classify the wife as a helpmate, I do not disagree with them because a helpmate has no full legal right or status eg. A driver mate has no right with the drive, he always take instruction from the driver and has no right to do certain things, on his own. Likewise roommate is not a tenant, therefore has no full right like a tenant. Therefore considerations which a tenant may receive, a roommate may not. In like manna helpmate is under subjection and not a contributor. The Holy Ghost is a helper and not a help mate and has authority. The wife helps the husband in his decision making and has authority, if she refuse to help nothing is achieved, because behind every successful man is a woman. She stands behind the husband to succeed in all that he undertakes, encourage the husband when he is discouraged. The wife does not take instruction from the husband to perform or know her duties in the house. So on behalf of the wives I reject the word helpmate in Jesus name. Helpmate is slavery and not be used in a civilized countries or democratic countries. Helpmate is referred to in underdeveloped countries or developing countries and not developed countries.Gen.2:18, Eph. 5:28.

5. Avoid cheats (adultery). The bible says any man or woman who commit adultery or cheats has no understanding about marriage (the reason why he or she marries). So before you marry, you should be taught to have a clear understanding of marriage else marriage is a blessing but lack of understanding can turn it to be curse for the couple. Prov.6:32-33 "Whoever commits adultery with a woman lack understanding. He who does so, destroy his own soul. Wounds and dishonor he will get. And his reproach will not be wiped away." Hebr. 13:4 "Marriage is honorable in all, and the bed undefiled but for fornicators and adulterers, God will judge." Prov. 18:22 "He who finds a wife finds a good thing. And obtains favor from the Lord." (1Cor 6:13, 16, 18-20.) Learning the ethics of marriage before the wedding is called pre-marital counseling. It is an academic lectures or lessons given to new couples wishing to marry. It is important to every young couple heading towards marriage and this is simply always before the marriage, which is given by an expect or qualified pastor of a church before the couple is joined together. This should have a maximum duration of three months depending upon the instruction (appointed periods) of the expect and a minimum duration of six weeks. It is advisable that married couples go for counseling called post-marital counseling, every two or three years after their wedding for at least one week and this will depend upon the couple to decide. This will make their marriage successful and whenever there is misunderstanding they can quickly identify the source of the misunderstanding. They can also see their counselor. With counseling the marriage is more secured because raising ones academic standard in marriage makes one understand the pros and cons of marriage which helps the couple to be committed to one another. Post-marital counseling helps couples to mend and repair the broken pillars and walls or the collapsing foundation of the marriage. Post-marital counseling is strength to every marriage.

6. Appreciate your wives effort to promote happiness in the house. Honor your wives. Husbands should dwell with their wives according to knowledge, behave wisely and give the wife honor, so that there will not be any hindrance against your prayers. Be

one mind together. Give them surprises and send them out to treat them, let the wives be part of them. 1Pet. 3:1, 8. "Likewise ye wives, be in subjection to your own husbands; that if any obey not the word they also may without the word be won by the conversation of the wives. Finally be ye all of one mind, having compassion one of another, love as brethren, be pitiful, be courteous." Apostle Peter is saying eg. when an illiterate is married to a literate, either the illiterate will conform to live a life style as the literate or the literate will conform to live a lifestyle of an illiterate. One will definitely be conformed or influenced to live the lifestyle of the other. So a husband or a wife who does not obey the word of God is easily influenced.

7. Wives honor husbands.1Pet.3:5-7. The wife must look on the first Christian women and live with their husbands. Those women were willed to live holy and they trusted God, meaning they gave their everything to the service of God, (money, strength, beauty etc.) and they subjected themselves to their husbands. Even Sarah went as far as calling her husband Abraham "Lord." The bible says the wives are the daughter of Sarah therefore the wives should imitate Sarah.

8. Do not render evil for evil, because the husband fail to fulfill her demands, she will refuse to talk to the husband, to have mutual relation him. 1Pet. 3:9; 1Cor. 1:3-5; 1Cor. 7: 5. As Christians we do not have to pay one another evil for evil, or bitterness with bitterness but do things that will bless one another. This bitterness situation will result in stress, leading to high blood pressure and complicating to diabetes and even stroke and finally premature death. If a couple desires to break their marriage by rebellion, death will take advantage to separate them. We have to know that we have been called for a mission to inherit, especially a well prepared blessing, let go all bitterness, outrage, anger, clamor and evil speeches, and completely put away in marriages these behaviors, and be as Christians or responsible citizens for world peace.

9. Encourage one another. Rom. 14:19. "Let us follow after things that make for peace and things which bring encouragement to

both couple. Two are better than one because they have a good reward for their labor. If one fall then one will lift up his fellow; But woe to him that is alone when he falls he had not another to help him up. If one prevails against him the two shall withstand him, for a three fold cord is not quickly broken."

10. Divorce is ruled out of marriage according to the Christian doctrine except death separate the couple, even that, if the wife or the husband is capable he or she can decide not to marry and live the rest of her life alone, cleaving unto thing of God. Luke 2:36. Fornication is the only violation which can be used as basis for divorce. Even that if the husband or the wife loves her or him, nothing prevent them from continuing with their marriage. 1Cor. 7:10-11; 1Cor. 7:39; Rom. 7:2-3; Matt. 5:31-32; Matt. 19:3-9; Matt. 22:28-32; Eph. 4:29-30.

CONCLUSION: Remember always that the wife is a precious gift from God and if a gift from God then she must be precious in the eyes of the husband. Prov. 18:22; 19:14; Prov. 31:10 - Who can find a virtuous wife? For her worth (price) is far above rubies.: virtuous wife is always behind her husband and strongly wish her husband's success, for behind every successful husband there is a virtuous wife. The wish of God for every marriage is to prosper but rebellion of God's word breaks up the marriage.; The husband should cherish and love and consider her as part of himself that's his body.

EXTRACT:

Prov. 18:22 Whoso find a wife finds a good thing and obtains favor of the Lord.

Prov. 19:14 House and riches are the inheritance of the fathers, and prudent wife is from the Lord.

Prov. 5:18-19 Let thy fountain be blessed and rejoice with the wife of thy youth. Let her be as the loving hind and pleasant roe; let her breasts satisfy thee at all times: and be thou ravished always with her love.

QUIZ:

QUESTION:

1. Why should a husband or a wife cheat?

ANSWER:

1. Love – lack of love, a stressful marriage- misunderstanding and confusion. Eph. 5:25; Col 3:19
2. Denial - 1Cor. 7:5 Defraud ye not one another, except it be with consent for a time, that ye may give yourselves to fasting and prayer; and come together again, that Satan tempt you not for your incontinency.
3. The grace of God - Pray for God's grace, (lack of God's grace is a hindrance) praying together and for one another. Rom. 5:1-2
4. Neatness: - Lack of neatness can be a hindrance, attract one another.
5. Lust - Sometimes, not that the husband or the wife does not love the other but they do that out of lust (pray seriously against lust, for lust is an unclean spirit). Jude 16; Rom. 13:14.
6. Unacceptable behavior:- Uncontrollable anger, violence, unreasonable talks not considering the damage it shall cause, and can put both parties under stress.

QUESTION:

2. Jesus did not marry and so the pastors and apostles, prophets, evangelists need not to marry and be like Jesus?

ANSWER:

1. Jesus is the creator of all women. A creator marrying His creation is degrading, it's like someone who marries his own daughter, it's taboo and abomination, Lev. 18:6. Man is a creation and can marry creation, a woman. 1Cor. 7:8-9 "I say therefore to the unmarried and widows, It is good for them if they abide even as I. But if they cannot contain, let them marry: it is better to marry

than to burn. But if by faith a woman or a man desire to be single for the sake of the Lord, he or she can do so."

2. But do not allow constitution or traditionalism to bind you from marrying and do evil stuff in secret, that's against Christianity.

IDLE WORDS

The bible advices us that the words that proceed out of the mouth of a person forms the boarders[coast] of your life. Therefore whatever you say with your mouth will surely come into reality in your life. Words are spirit therefore once a word is spoke unto a person it mixes with the spiritual pattern of the person and gradually draws the pattern of the object, which becomes the ghost of that object and completely create that object to be the boarders of that person's life. When an architect wants to put up a building, he first imagines it and then put it on paper that forms the ghost, the blue print and with the ghost he will determine the cost of the project, then it is put into physical realm and we see with our eyes a mighty building. Curse, blessings, and prophecy is like that. So once we say something unto a person it is spiritually inscribed in his life which begins to rule his life afterwards. In John 3:11-13. says, "Verily, verily, I say unto thee, we speak that we do know, and testify that we have seen; and ye received not our witness. If I have told you earthly things, and ye believe not, how shall ye believe, if I tell you of heavenly things? And no man hath ascended up to heaven, but he that came down from heaven, even the son of man which is in heaven." There are things which are very difficult to believe because they are spiritual, it is descend, only by the spirit of discernment those things could be comprehended.

In Mark 7:15. "There is nothing from without a man, that entering into him can defile him; but the things which come out of him, those are they that defile the man." Jesus continue to explain in Mark 15:18-23. "Do ye not perceive, that whatsoever thing from without entereth into the man, it cannot defile him. Because it entereth not into his heart, but into the belly, and goeth out into the draught, purging all meat? And said that which cometh out of the man that defile the man. For from within, out of the heart of men, proceed evil thoughts, adulteries, fornication, murders, thefts, covetousness wickedness, deceit, lasciviousness, an evil eye, blasphemy, pride, foolishness: All these evil things come from within, and defile the man." So man by the above acts produce evil spirits into the world. So in Matt. 5:21-22 "Ye have heard that it was said by them of old time, Thou shall not kill: and whosoever shall kill shall be in danger of the judgment. But I say unto you that whosoever is angry with his brother without a cause shall be in danger of the judgment: and whosoever shall say to his brother 'RACA' shall be in danger of the council: but whosoever shall say, 'THOU FOOL' shall be in danger of hell fire." Jesus came to eliminate evil spirits because they are dangerous in the life of man, so He was casting them out and make sure they do not live, and if mankind should use violence evil word to cause the production of demons such person will face the council and the hell fire (meaning you will face God the father, God the son and God the Holy ghost) as the council and be delivered to Satan as the hell fire. That is the punishment and the consequences of bleeding unclean spirits into the world. It is very sad to hear a mother tells her own child 'stupid,' injecting the spirit of stupidity into a child conceived nine months, to torment the child, forgetting the pain she went through for the nine months. It's just sad.

People insult God, they insult Christ and insult the Holy ghost but the bible warns that they should be careful for what comes out of their mouth, because it will definitely bring curse upon them.

Matt. 12 31-32. "Wherefore I say unto you, All manner of sin and blasphemy shall be forgiven unto men: the blasphemy against the holy Spirit shall not be forgiven unto men. And whosoever speaketh a word against the son of man, it shall be forgiven him: but whosoever speaketh against the Holy Ghost, it shall not be forgiven him, neither in this world, neither in the world to come." The new testament again says: in vs. 36-37 that every idle word that men shall speak they shall give account thereof in the day of judgment. For by thy word thou shall be justified, and by thy word thou shall be condemned. Lev.24:15-16. "And thou shall speak unto the children of Israel, saying whosoever curseth his God shall bear his sin. And he that blasphemeth the name of the Lord, he shall surely be put to death, and all the congregation shall certainly stone him: as well the stranger, as he that is born in the land, who blasphemeth the name of the Lord, shall be put to death." Blasphemy against the Holy ghost is very serious offence and God warns mankind to refrain from that, because of it's bleeding of unclean spirits and the curse it brings unto mankind. For that Christ destroyed evil spirit and gave us power to continue to destroy them and their works. In Luke 9:1. "Then He called his disciples together, and gave them power and authority over all devils and to cure diseases." And Luke 10:8-9. "And into whatsoever city ye enter, and they receive you, eat such thing as are set before thee, and heal the sick that are therein, and say unto them, the kingdom of God is come nigh unto you." Christ has given us power over serpents, and scorpions and over all the power of the enemy but we have to use this power carefully. These evil spirits or unclean spirits don't cease trying, if one plan fails they try another plan, they go to churches, to the markets, grave yards, in the sea, holes, in the air, jungles etc. but the bible says we are complete in Him which is the head of all principalities and powers. Jesus told us exactly where to instruct the demon to go, revealing the power of the word of God and encourage us to be specific in our prayer with authority given to us over demons. When we tell the mountains to move, we should tell it where to go. Matt. 21:21-22. Else it will be loitering and possess an innocent person or will not move at all, because it does not know where to go, Matt. 12:43-45. We do not have to play with the enemy.

Idle words fuses with ones ability of determination and encourages various difficulties. People talk their difficulties because there is no sufficient space in the mind for that knowledge of difficulties. It is unwise to tell ones secret to one who is not necessary to be told. Ones progress is a secret affair so if you want to progress keep your mouth shut and keep your eyes and ears opened and do what you have to do. What comes out of your mouth forms the boarders of your life so be careful of the words that issues out of your mouth.

Idle Words brings the denial of God's help in time of need and judgment. Words have power, every word carries power and once the word is spoken power will be released. The power behind the word is converted to a spirit which will possess the person upon whom the word was spoken, and in matter of time, the spirit will begin to manifest in that person. The person's life style will carry the image of that word spoken upon him.

2Timothy 2:16. "But shun profane and idle babblings for they will increase to more ungodly."

Words can cause terrible damage or cause wonderful good things or healing. Good words that come out of the heart cause manifestation outside likewise bad words.

Jesus said in John 6:63. "It is the Spirit which gives life, the flesh profit nothing. The words that I speak to you are Spirit and they are life." Because Jesus was speaking good words, they are spirit that carry life and give salvation.

Proverbs 4:23 Keep your heart with all diligence, For out of it springs the issues of life.

People with heart troubles are always confused because the heart is the instrument for understanding and is disorganized. Bitterness escalates heart troubles and results in hatred.

Matt. 12:36-37. "But I say to you that for every idle word men may speak, they will give account of it in the day of judgment. For by your word you will be justified, and by your word you will be condemned." So each and everyone shall account for the words that we spoke as idle as they are.

Roman 6:16. "Do you not know that to whom you present yourself slaves to obey, you are that ones slaves whom you obey whether of sin leading to death or of obedience leading to righteousness."

What is secret is that which consists of your Christian faith. Words could be deadly or could be fruitful, a life giver. **As new Christian or a baby in Christ, you expect God to honor your desires and God understands that because that's the order of babies, but for a matured Christian your expectation is to obey and do the will of God and that's what makes you a Christian.**

Ephesians 4:29-31. "Let no corrupt word proceed out of your mouth but what is good for necessary edification, that may impact grace to the hearer. And do not grieve the Holy Spirit of God, by whom you were sealed for the day of redemption. Let all bitterness, wrath, anger, clamor and evil speaking be put away from you with all malice."

Lev. 24:14. "Take outside the camp him who has cursed then let all who heard him lay their hands on his heard, and let all congregation stone him."

In the time of Moses those who curse or speak idle words are eliminated from the face of the earth. But for the grace of Jesus Christ, we live. So stop cursing.

Colossians 3:8-9. "But now you yourselves are to put off all these, anger, wrath, malice, blasphemies, **filthy language out of your mouth.** Do not lie to one another since you have put of the old man with his deeds."

SALVATION

REASON FOR SALVATION

When man sinned and God separated from man, man began to search for a way to get back to God. Then man began to practice good works, it did not worked out for him. Philosophy became a means of modest principle of character, it also could not bring man to God. Then philosophy led to religion which began the approach of drawing man to God, bringing out priest, prophets, men of God and the church began. Out of the church came women of God, then finally God interceded and brought His Son Our Lord Jesus Christ for the final completion of the reconciliation. Our Lord Jesus Christ was sent to the world to absolve the sins which separated God and Man, and Jesus Christ became the bridge through which man could get access of having contact with God. Man therefore turned from sin, cross through Jesus Christ to have connection with God. This shows that salvation does not depend upon man's good works, modest principle of life, or philosophy and the power of the mind, but depend upon the love and the mercy of God and the grace of Our Lord Jesus Christ who paid a ransom by the sacrifice of His life and the shedding of His blood on the cross. In the beginning the church comprise of a family with the father or the husband as the priest eg. Adam Gen.4:24; Jacob Gen. 28:13-15; Abraham Gen. 12:1-3; Noah Gen. 6:18. which had no evangelical base or purpose. But with the advent of Moses as he was called in the wilderness as God revealed Himself to him (Moses) for the salvation of the Church and the twelve assemblies. This was the twelve tribes of Israel which became an organization of a nation. under the leadership of Moses Exo. 19:6. A theocracy which involved the complete life of a nation, the political life, the social life and the religious life. To this we say God was the ruler, the commander- in- chief and even in this new testament era God is, because He is the King of Kings and the Lord Of Lords. Then came Christ who was sent by the Father upon the Jews whom they rejected, and the rejection created a new advent for the world salvation, which raise the Pentecostal era, the immerging of Christianity, the Christ churches and its institutions, as ministries. Hence salvation is to set free or delivered from destruction, failure or harmful situation.

The following names has the same meaning as salvation. Instead of saying salvation, one can choose to say redemption, or regeneration, or mystery or rescue or born again. They all mean the same thing.

Mystery: rescue beyond the knowledge of man; confessing the name of Jesus Christ and believing in his death, resurrection and ascension. Eph. 3:9 And to make plain to everyone the administration of this mystery which for ages pass was kept hiding in God which created all thing by Jesus Christ.

Redemption: To remove someone from danger. Or To take back. Eph. 1:7 In Him we have redemption, through His blood the forgiveness of sins in accordance with the riches of His grace that lavished on us with all wisdom and understanding.

Regeneration: Subject to spiritual renewal. Matt. 19:28 And Jesus said unto them, verily I say unto you, that ye which had followed Me in the regeneration [the renewal of all things] when the Son of man shall sit on His throne of His glory ye also shall sit upon twelve thrones judging the twelve tribes of Israel.

Rescue: To save or release one from custody under captivity. Acts 23:27 This man was seized by the Jews and they were about to kill him but I came with my troop and rescued him for I have learned that he is a Roman citizen.

Born Again: To be made again without sin. [rebirth or recycle]. John 3:3 Jesus answered and said unto him, verily, verily, I say unto you unless a man be born again, he cannot see the kingdom of God.

MEANING FOR SALVATION:- Salve is a medicinal substance applied to the skin to smoothing it to make the skin fresh and new, and God can use any substance [the word of God, water, olive oil, coconut water, water from the sea, water from the river ect. to make one new or give rebirth]

2Kings 5:14. This is physical medicine. But in the Christian sense Salvation is the saving of a person from sin or saving of a person from danger or difficulty, destruction or evil, a spiritual medicine. If you live in sin, you live in danger because you become vulnerable to the attacks of Satan. The bible says in Prov. 14:12. "There is a way that seem right to a man, but it's end is the way of death." And Proverbs 16:2. "All ways of a man are pure in his eyes, but the Lord weighs the spirit." There are so many people attending church who are not saved, and it's all the same good. Therefore, for someone to obtain salvation, that person must first have repentance, and his sins forgiven then be baptized and he or she is saved. Salvation is a free gift, which every human being must receive, no matter who you are or where you came from. Salvation leads to an everlasting life and redeems us from destruction, therefore we have been retrieved from the physical world to the spiritual world. This salvation is only found in Jesus Christ and nobody else. Acts 4:12. Salvation is beyond the knowledge of man which is a mystery. Eph. 3:9. "And to make all men see what is the fellowship of the mystery which from the beginning of the world hath hid in God, who created all things by Jesus Christ." The bible says it was hidden in God and was released to Christ. When the dominion was taken from man, all rights was taken from him and man lost the rightful ownership but God knew what would happen in future so He well protected it, the most precious ornament of life. If salvation had been lost, Jesus wouldn't have come to save us. Salvation is more powerful than dominion. Salvation was so precious to God that he did not leave it with anybody, but kept it in himself. It was simple because salvation was the definite thing of God for the redemption of mankind, therefore it was kept in a highly secured environment, which was inside God. God knows the future and knows the deep thing of every human being, therefore He placed a very high security on salvation. Salvation is a miracle by itself and **supersedes** all miracles and subdues all miracles. It supersedes healing and supersedes casting out of demons. When man sinned and died in spirit and realized his mistake and sought for a reconciliation, God also tried to find a way to regenerate man. Ezekiel 22:30. "And I sought for a man (the mediator of the new covenant) among them, that should make up the hedge, and stand in the gap before Me for the land, that I should not destroy it but I found none." The Father for his wonderful love for mankind sought for a propitiator.

31

Do you remember Abraham pleading with God to consider the righteous among the people and God saying there is none among them, from fifty to one there was none except Abraham himself and God tried to use Isaac and Abraham pleaded for Isaac to live, God will bring a lamb. Gen. 22:1-8.

FUNCTION OF SALVATION:- Salvation is gift from God to all humans without going to the mountains to spend forty days and forty nights without food or water, without taking shower and sleeping on the rock in the mountains or forty years of slavery for exchange. Our savior and Lord Jesus Christ, the God of salvation has taken it upon Himself and suffered that for us. Gal. 4:4-5. But when the fullness of the time was come God sent forth his son made of a woman made under the law, to redeem them that were under the law that we might receive the adoption of son. Jesus reveal his purpose. Jesus came from million of miles, from heaven to the earth, left all his glory as a king, a ruler, as living God, perform miracles to confirm his majesty, to open the eyes of the blind, cast out demons, to let the dump talk and the lame walk, walk on the sea (only God can walk on the sea) because Gen. 1:1 says the spirit of God was at the creation moving on the waters. The bible says the people saw Jesus as he was walking on the sea as Ghost (spirit) and they were afraid. In John 3:1-6 Nicodemus a priest came to Jesus by night because he was protecting his position filled with power consciousness and completely in the flesh, he was so much attached to the worldly position and did not understand what Jesus said because his intention was to see more miracle but Jesus rather gave him salvation. To be born of water is repentance from deep within you and means to be baptized with water and that's what John the Baptist did. He baptized the people with water unto repentance and to be born of the spirit is the acceptance of the Holy Spirit and His tongues. And once you are born of the spirit your speech, your works, your character, everything that you do must display Christ and the Holy Spirit., You cannot have salvation without repentance. Once we receive salvation we are dead to sin and we become conscious of sin. 1Peter 1:23. "Being born again not of corruptible seed but of incorruptible by the word of God which liveth and abide forever."

1Peter 2:24 Who His own self bear our sins in His own body on the tree, that we being dead to sin, should live unto righteousness. By who's strips ye are healed. King David said in Psalm 119:176. "I have gone astray like a lost sheep, seek thy servant, for I do not forget thy commandments." David was pleading with God to restore him spiritually but people of this modern era are much blessed with this free gift.

PURPOSE OF SALVATION:- Luke. 19:10. "For the son of man is come to seek and to save that which is lost." Here it was not man that got lost, but something spiritual, so precious got lost. Something which is higher than man which can be possessed by man, angel even Satan. The bible declares in: Gen. 1:26 HAVE DOMINION. So when the dominion was taken from man, man got lost. Meaning the dominion was greater than man. Without the dominion man is spiritually dead in this world. What makes man precious is the dominion. The jealous of Satan against man is because of the dominion. In Isaiah 14:12-14. Satan claiming to be above everything and, above God. But when Satan saw the dominion with man because the dominion is the power behind the word which cause Heaven and Earth to be in existence, which also give path to man. He became aggressive and device devices against man. Rev. 12:7-11. Says the angels waged war against him and he was cast down and the saints conquered him by the blood of the Lamb and the word of their testimony. Job.9:24. The world is given into the hands of the wicked one. Because he has blinded the eyes of the legal owners. And in. Gen. 3:2-6. Satan made a legal agreement with Eve for the exchange with fruit –man did not know the value of the dominion at that time and gave it out for food, Good for food – to make a woman beautiful; a tree to be desired to make one wise – something that carries intelligence and wisdom; Pleasant to the eyes – to be admired by men.. Luke. 4:6. Satan made show of the power delivered onto him by Adam before Christ. And in: Matt. 28:18. Jesus also made show of the power given to him by the Father both on earth and in heaven (Eph.3:4-5). Satan saw that the power given to him was low so there he was conquered and caste out of the world again this time by Jesus. (John. 12:31) Now is the judgment of the world, now shall the prince of the world be cast out. John 14:30. Here after I will not talk with you for the prince of this world cometh and hath nothing in me. Satan took the world as his own property, but blessed be to the living God that He had retrieved it from the grip of Satan. And this was the first defeat of Satan by Christ. Colo. 2:13-15. Christ had quickened us together with him and forgiven us our trespasses. Blotting out our sins and took it out and nail it on the cross. Christ therefore spoil principalities and powers and made show of his victory openly triumphing over them in it. Colo. 2:8. Jesus Christ now warns us to be careful that no man spoil us through philosophy and vain deceit after the logic and traditions of the world and not after Christ. Now the bible says; Colo: 2:9 We are complete in Christ, we now have all the weapons, the armor, the ammunitions to fight Satan and his kingdom. Confirmed in, Mark 16:16-18. Those of us who believe and are baptized, shall be saved: but those that believe not shall be damned. Salvation of man was a great war between Jesus Christ and Satan and Christ won the battle. He made show of it before the whole world and before mankind, and saw him rose from death of crucifixion, confusing the devil and scaring him and his host.

PACKAGE:- And these signs shall follow them that believe: In my name 1. shall they cast out devils, 2. they shall speak with new tongues, 3. they shall take up serpent. 4. they shall drink deadly things like juju, voodoo, talismans. Idols, gods unknowingly, they will have no effect on them and 5. they shall lay hands on the sick and they will recover. 6.We have received salvation and saved through Christ. 7. We can now come to the father. 8. We are now children of God. 9. We can ask Him what we want and He will surely give us.10. That we also may go out to spread His word and win souls unto Him. 11. Satan is made a looser and God has won.

BENEFIT:- In Psalm. 51:12. Restore unto me the joy of thy salvation. David searched for this package of the salvation and did not receive but Christ has delivered this package automatically unto Christians. 1Cor. 6:20. The Lord Jesus Christ paid an expensive price to retrieve us. Eph. 2:12. We had no hope with God in the world but 13. We are now brought near to God by the blood of Christ. 14. The Lord Jesus Christ is our peace, our shepherd and had broken the middle wall of partition between God and man, and God is now visible and face to face with man.

BAPTISM

What is baptism? Baptism means complete immersion or total immersion. It is a ceremony marking a person's admission into the Christian congregation by immersion in water at an age when a person is old enough to understand what this ceremony means, knowing and understanding good and evil. It is the new testament baptism. John 3:1-8. An infant can be presented for dedication to the Lord but not for baptism. Luke 2:21-22

Key Scripture:-1.1Cor. 12:13 2. Hebr. 6:1-2 3. Matt. 28:19; 4.Luke 11:13 5. Matt. 3:11-12

Institution of baptism: (Establishment) Matt. 28:19; Mark 16:15-16. It was a commandment from Jesus.

TYPES OF BAPTISM:-

There are four types of baptism that a person must receive to be declared a child of God. Each of these baptism is very important for one's admission as a Christian. These are:-

1. Baptism by one spirit into one body ---Public confession (repentance acceptance, or baptism of repentance. Acts 3:38; Matt. 3:1-2; Matt. 3:11; It is the spirit of submission, humility.)
2. Baptism in water ---Position (where one declares his position in or give self to Christ. Acts 8:29-39.)
3. Baptism in the Holy Spirit.---Power (Acts 4:8-13.)
4. Baptism with Fire ---Holiness (standing alone spirit. Acts 16:22-26 Acts 7:55-60.)

1. Baptism into one body:- Rom. 10:9-10. Whenever a person without Christ surrenders to Christ, the Holy Spirit enters that person's life. Rom. 8:9 But ye are not in the flesh but in the spirit, if indeed the spirit of God dwells in you. Now if anybody does not have the spirit of Christ, he is not his. As soon as one is drawn by the Holy

Spirit into the body of Christ, he becomes a new born spiritual baby. John 6:44,65Eph. 2:4-9, Eph.4:4-5, Eph.3:9, Rom. 10:9-10, Acts. 2:38-39. It is the symbol of the believer's identification with Lord Jesus Christ in his death, burial and resurrection. It is an open and public confession of the Lordship of Jesus Christ.

2. Baptism in water:- There are four kinds of this baptism in use, Sprinkling, pouring, effusion and immersion. But one thing we have to know is the term baptism which means "TO DIP" that is total immersion. Since baptism is the identification of the death, burial and resurrection of our Lord Jesus Christ therefore Sprinkling, pouring and effusion cannot satisfy the purpose of Baptism of the new testament. John 3:23-27 Mark 1: 9-10, Acts 8:36-39. It is a change of mind, which makes one to put away the old things and walk in the works of Christ. Water baptism is the outward sign of repentance and forgiveness of sins through faith in Jesus Christ not through the performing of the baptism. It is the physical operation expressing our faith in God.

UNDER THIS BAPTISM ARE:-

1. The institution of water baptism.
2. The mode of water baptism.
3. The significance of water baptism.
4. Subjects of water baptism

THE INSTITUTION OF WATER BAPTISM:-

This is the time and command of establishing this kind of baptism. It marks when this baptism was established, how it was instituted, why it was established and what it is. Matt. 3:16, Matt. 28:-19, Acts 2:-38,41.

MODE OF WATER BAPTISM [KINDS]:-

SPRINKLING [CONSECRETION]:- This is done where water is very scarce eg. In the desert. It is an emergency baptism, that could be done to secure the member's faith in Christ as a Pentecostal believer or in the charismatic churches, that person must be re-baptized by immersion in water.

POURING [CONSECRETION]:- This kind of baptism is applied where the river has a high force of current or the water is under high pressure and could not be entered, or where there are no rivers, lakes or ponds. This is done with bucket from a well or where the river cannot be entered and poured upon the recipient and is acceptable water baptism.

EFFUSION [CONSECRETION]:- By means of gushing forth on tap of the pipe borne water, the recipient must be re-baptized in a river because it does not satisfy the new testament baptism.

EMMERSION:-[TO DIP] This is the Christ recommended new testament baptism symbolizing the Death, burial and resurrection of Jesus Christ. Matt. 3:16:- Jesus when he was baptized went up straightaway out of the water and lo the heavens were opened unto him and he saw the spirit of God descending like a dove and lighting upon him. Mark 16:15-16. "And he said unto them, go ye unto all the world and preach the gospel to every creature. He that believes and baptized shall be saved but he that believes not shall be damned." So Jesus gave the bishops, apostles, pastors, evangelists, missionaries, Archbishops the mandate or the power to baptize. Matt. 28:19. In the name of the father and of the son and of the Holy Ghost shall the converts of the new testament be Baptized.

Acts 2:38-41. "Peter said unto them repent and be baptized every one of you in the name of Jesus Christ for the remission of sins and ye shall receive the gift of the Holy Ghost." They believed, repented, confessed and were baptized. Have faith in Christ that he was crucified, Dead, buried and resurrected. It's just that.

SIGNIFICANCE OF WATER BAPTISM:- The purpose of water baptism:- It is the symbol of the believer's identification with Jesus Christ in his death, burial and resurrection. It is an open and public confession of the lordship of the Lord Jesus Christ and acceptance of the Christian faith. Rom. 6:3-4. "Know ye not that so many of us as were baptized into Jesus Christ were baptized into his death. Therefore we are buried with him by baptism unto death, like as Christ was raised up from the death by the glory of the Father even so we also should walk in newness of life."

Colossians 2:9-12. "For in him dwells all the fullness of the Godhead bodily. And ye are complete in him which is the head of all principalities and powers. In whom also ye are circumcised with the circumcision made without hands, inputting off the body of the sins of the flesh by the circumcision of Christ. Buried with Him in baptism, where in also ye are risen with Him through the faith the operation of God who had raised Him from the dead." SUBJECT OF WATER BAPTISM:-Baptism is saved for those who are prepared and believe that salvation is the only way to come back to God. This new testament baptism comprise of the following:-

1. Those who receive the word Acts 2:41.
2. Those who have received the spirit. Acts 10:47,44; 16:34; 18:8; 1Cor.1:16
3. Those who can hear the word. Acts 10:44.
4. Those who hear and believe. Acts 16:30-34.

These are those qualified to be baptized.

Baptism in water is a spiritual act or operation leading to the spiritual truth in Christ. In water baptism we are in effect sharing with Christ his death, burial and resurrection. Rom. 6:3-7, Gal. 2:20, Col. 2:12.

We must be baptized in water because:- 1. Jesus has commanded us to do so. Matt. 28:19. 2. It shows our conscience towards God. 1Pet. 3:21. 3. It's something Jesus himself did. Matt. 3:13-17. 4. The faith of the early churches was based on this. Acts 2:41, Acts 10:47-48. 5. It represent the cleansing of sins, by the blood and word of God Acts 22:16. 6. It create joy in heaven, and increase the capacity of God's kingdom. 7. We are transform from the world and removed from the kingdom of Satan. John 15:19

3.HOLY SPIRIT BAPTISM:- This baptism is the promise from our Lord Jesus Christ. The Holy Spirit is a gift and is not bought with money, it is a free gift to all who believe. Acts 1:8. We do not have to be confused with the Holy Ghost baptism and the anointing of the God. The anointing brings the casting out of demons, performing of healing and miracles. But the Holy Spirit baptism helps the believer to lead a righteous life and take responsibility in the work of God. This baptism brings forth the gift of the Holy Spirit- that's the anointing to glorify the Lord. 1Cor. 12:7-11. It gives boldness. Acts 2:14-15, 4:31;Rom.8:15-16. It also increases our love for the word of God and gives understanding. John 16:13; 1Cor.2:9-16. This baptism is received by faith (Gal.3:2-5) it is not struggle for, agonized, begged for, or bargained. It is a free gift of the Lord Jesus to his disciples to enable them walk as he did. Luke 11:11-13

BAPTISM WITH FIRE:- This baptism builds a magnetic field around the believer to repel the attacks (missiles). We become vessels more able to fulfill what God has planed for our lives. God has chosen to use our circumstances and the pressures of life to achieve this process of purifying our lives. Like the chaff (matt. 3:12) be burnt by unquenchable fire, we must be prepared to withstand. We must learn to take advantage of these pressures. Without these pressures we never be as God wants us to be to fulfill our full potential in Christ. Matt. 26:67. Matt. 27:27-31. We ask God to change us but when the pressures come we pray to God to remove it. 1Pet.1:7. (1Pet.4:12-19, 2Tim.2:3, Rev. 2:10).

CONFESSION:-I lift up my hands and accept Jesus Christ as my Lord and savior. I believe that Jesus Christ is the son of God who was sent by the father unto the world who shed his blood at Calvary and cleansed me and gave up his life that I may receive salvation. Lord I lift up my hands and confess my sins before you that you will forgive me. I will worship you with the rest of my life. In Jesus name. Amen.

CHAPTER TWO

Understanding Fasting (Points For Fasting)

Introduction:- Fasting is the greatest of the amour of God delivered to Christians for the well being of the Christian. It is the first and foremost in the life of a believer to seek the face of God. Fasting has been in application not in our modern days but has been in existence time immemorial. It worked for our fathers and it also works for us. Whether you believe it or not, it works. Fasting based upon the word of God and by God's direction.

Memory Verse: Esther 4:16 Go, gather all the Jews who are present in Shushan {abundant lilies, the capital of Elam (eternity) the son of Shem and the grandson of Noah} and fast for me neither eat nor drink for three days night and day. My maids and I will fast likewise. And so I will go to the king which is against the law, and if I perish I perish. Mark 9:29 This kind can come forth by nothing but by prayer and fasting.

Points for Fasting

1. Fasting is the ceremony in the air against principalities, rulers and powers and agents of spiritual wickedness. It is the highest activity in ones life. It is the basis of ones spiritual life for a new direction. Acts 10:30, 9 - 10.
2. Fasting brings humbleness before God. It is sowing to the spirit to reaping the fruit of the spirit. Psalms 35:13 1Kings 21:27-29
3. Fasting brings righteousness to improve our relationship with God and enable us to communicate with Him and for God to hear us to obtain his mercy and grace. Joel 2:12 Matt. 5:6.
4. Fasting brings the anointing of the Holy Ghost. Acts 13:2-3, Acts 10:9-10. .When we have the anointing of God we shall see the mind of God and He will reveal things to us.
5. Fasting is the magnetic weapon for every Christian. Exodus 34:28-30.
6. We fast to magnetize the demon behind the problem for which we are offering prayer into the arena to be conquered. If you fear fasting you can never have breakthrough. Matt. 4:2-4

7. Fasting means asking the devil to bow before God. eg. authorities are forced by hanger strikers to do their will for them. Dan. 10:2-5 The enemy surenders and God's hand become great.

8. Fasting should be to the Lord. Zech. 7:5, Luke 2:37, Isaiah 58:3-10, Matt. 6:16-18.

9. Fasting means mourning, when we fast to the Lord the Lord will take control of the situation, you will be comforted. Matt. 5:4 Blessed are they that mourn for they shall be comforted. Dan. 10:2-3

10. Fasting is part of our spiritual warfare as it was with Jesus. Matt. 4:1-11.

11. Fasting is part of our preparation for the service in the spiritual development as well as defeating Satan. Neh. 1:4.when you fast you are demonstrating your love for God and your readiness to walk with Him

12. Fasting gives us strength and privilege for the tremendous calling of the Lord. Acts 14:23.

13. Fasting opens up to the spiritual world (for identification of good and bad). Ester 4:1-7.

14. Fasting facilitate the infusion of spiritual energy and life. 1 Kings 19:8-9.

15. Fasting present the body as a vehicle for prayer. Exo. 34:28, 33:11

16. Fasting in itself offer prayer to God. 2Sam. 12:16

17. Fasting drains away unbelief and opens up more spiritual insight.

18. Fasting alert the spirit to be more aware of the world forces of darkness and spiritual forces of wickedness.

19. Fasting expose us to God, giving God the appeal and commission to change us to what he wills and to use us in a more dynamic way. Isaiah 58:5-10 Fasting also expose the gift of God in us.

20. Fasting works in lifting our prayer to God. Mark 9:29.This kind can come forth by nothing but by prayer and fasting.

21. Fasting opens the door of positive spiritual power in the Holy Ghost. Matt. 4:2-11.

22. Fasting acknowledges the true source of life. And helps us to have dominion over our physical body to enter into the spiritual realm.

23. Fasting releases revelations of Jesus and power in peoples lives. Acts 10:9-10.

24. Fasting brings spiritual issues to surface and purges the body of the poisons. eg. hatred, wickedness, murder, idolism, adultery, witchcraft, fornication, etc. Acts 9:9.

Definition:- Fasting means waiting on the Lord in the new testament and in the old testament, it means mourning. it means abstaining from food and drinks, sex, etc. Fasting is casual and not permanent abstinence, therefore children of God should not fear to fast. Fasting becomes necessary when everything has failed, strength, wisdom, effort, knowledge, family, friends, nation, etc. concerning our success besetting sin, fear, problems, demonic attacks, wars and besiege. Is. 40:28-29. We should not fast by motivation of self interest and self seeking because God hates that. Fasting and praying should be God initiated and ordained if it is to be effective, ministering unto the Lord yields good results.

Personal Benefit

Fasting is more of a tonic than medicine. In times past fasting formed part of the medical profession. Under the physical condition it is very good as a cleanser. It helps the mind or the brain to have it's proper realization deserved for all future activities. Your body begins to renew in the fullness of it's beauty after fasting.. Emotions or senses- become less burden which reflects in the face by the peace of God, in your heart. Phil. 4:6-7. As a result this good health is experienced, Dan. 1:15 and also Is. 58:8-9. with pure conscience towards God (righteousness), God rewards the individual (Matt. 6:17-18; Lk. 4:2).

Major Purpose Of Biblical Fasting

In whatever fasting you project yourself, the supreme intention should be the central focus. eg.

To change God's mind. Jonah 3:5-10 To be heard of on high to glorify God Ezra 8:21-23

To free the captives Is. 58:6 To deliver the oppressed Is. 49:24-25 For revelation Dan. 9:2-3

To avoid flesh pots of Egypt; the Israelites complaining of hanger. Ex. 16:3; Eve deceived, Gen. 3:6; Noah was intoxicated and resulted in cursing Ham his son Gen. 9:20-21; Israelites spoke against God. Num. 21:5; Num. 11:4-5; 2 Pet. 2:18-20, Consequences 1 Cor. 10:7-10

To cleanse the body 1 Cor. 9:27; (consequences: to minimize too much eating and desire for sex) Jer. 5:7

Avoid neglect of God Deut. 32:15-19; solution Rom. 13:14 and For health and healing Dan. 1:15, Isa.58:8

The Three Kinds of Fasting: There three kinds of fasting in use. Absolute, Normal, and Partial. The selection of the kind of fasting depends on the type of situation to be handled. People pay some men of God to fast for them. Even though it might work, the member is only helping the Levitt to strengthen his relationship with God and that member will never have intimate relationship with God. Know that hiring someone to bring you to God does not work always, it might work sometimes and sometimes it might not work but the Levitt reap the benefit.

Absolute

This kind of fasting is devoid of any food or drink for whatsoever. And the maximum duration according to medical advice is three days in order to maintain normal health. This is normally done in most dangerous and critical situations in the life of a child of God and the answer is obvious because God is faithful. The people involved mostly dwell on supernatural plain or are ministered to by the angels. In fasting we are healed of infirmities. Depending on the seriousness of the problem you can fast for three days straight without food and water and after that you will even feel more healthier followed by miracles. Esther 4:16. This could be done by any normal human being. But there are situations where some people fast for straight seven days dry or even fourteen straight dry days. There are instances where people fast for straight thirty [30] or forty [40] day and night without food or water. Moses did it Exodus 24:18 and Exodus 34:28. Elijah went without food for forty days 1Kings 19:8, Jesus the Son of God set us an example by fasting for forty. Luke 4:2. In fasting for thirty days or forty day dry the person is elevated and some even visit heaven and come with testimonies. Some also receive unimaginable gifts for the glory of God. Such fasting is very difficult but will depend upon the readiness of our heart. When Jesus was about to go to the cross He said Father My heart is ready. If the heart is ready for God, all will be possible. The scripture said those who will endure, to the end they will be saved. I have not seen any one who fasted for forty days without food or water but I have seen people who fasted for straight seven days dry and fourteen days straight dry. Even a close family member of my, fasted for seven days straight dry without food nor water. I am witness. You should be encouraged that this will be followed by a major miracle.

Normal

In this type fasting we normally restrict ourselves to fluid. It is normally wise, to consume enough of fluid or water to suffice and solicit cleansing and tone- up of the whole bodily system, and this is good because it has the effect of flushing out your kidneys and generally cleaning out the body. Counting on the thirst from the fasting and taking large quantities of fluid to your satisfaction does not make your fasting normal and may not yield the result you may be expecting, this can even cause discomfort and will surely jeopardize your mission of fast. Another thing to aim at is sufficient exercise to bring out the accumulated sweat and impurities from the blood stream, if the aim is to benefit the physical body, for blood being the magnetic agent in the body's purification system. Under every spiritual operation, even mental or whatever, fasting is very indispensable agent.

To be specific Pure water, fruit juice, water with little lemon and honey are kind of purifying agents but it is wise to take just tea or coffee since both are very strong stimulants for more physical benefits at the end of the fast in each day. This fasting is usually from 6:00am to 6:00pm, a twelve hour duration. But most believers take it from7:00pm to 6:00pm a twenty three hour duration tested to be very effective. It could be three days, seven days, fourteen day, twenty-one days, thirty days or forty days depending on the situation and your tendency to cope with.

Partial

In this type of fasting you eat something in between within the twelve hours but you do not eat much. Daniel 10:2-3 and 1Cor. 8:8. By eating something does not mean you can eat at any time or the way you want but you should have a systematic procedure which may have a fixed continuous time interval. This will show that you are fasting eg. At 10.00am you can take a cup of tea with slice of bread and at 3:00 pm a cup of coffee or tea and at 7:00pm you can take a small bowl of soup or vegetable soup not necessary this but your choice with apple, or can also depend on fruits. Usually this situation is granted for sick people who are eager to break up their sicknesses and have their liberty. You can also take a cup of water with the food. It all depend upon the capacity and the faith of intention of the believer.

Uncomfortable Reaction

People who do not fast often face uncomfortable situations and normally experience some type of physical reactions in the initial stages of the fasting. It's basically because of our chronic habits or our eating life style. The most popular unpleasant physical reactions are headaches, very severe dizziness and sometimes stomach pain. This is because you are liberating your body to do a lot of clean-up screening which is needed to be done. Where hunger is so severe, you have to lay down to rest and pray by taking the amour of God in resistance against the tricks of the devil. Use the shield of faith to quench all his flaming darts and wiles. Also with the sword of the spirit declare victory of the Lord over the enemy. Use it as is written in Matt. 4:4 on the devil by Our Lord Jesus Christ. Elderly people must also be careful when they fast, they may experience physical reaction, more especially when they break the fast. Under no circumstance should a believer break a fast with cold foods. Do not drink or eat cold foods and then eat or drink hot or warm food or drink over it. You will experience very serious uncomfortable situation. Why? The stomach and the intestines are already contracted and once the cold liquid gets in, they over contract and squeeze or cramp, and as a result causing stomach pain. Now when a hot or warm food or liquid is placed over the cold food, there will be instant expansion of the cold food or drink and can cause severe stomach pain and can end the fasting. Always break the fast with some warm drink or food or foods or under normal atmospheric temperature not in winter.

Preparing to Fast and During Fasting

Positive faith based on the promised reward. Refusing to fast is refusing to receive the promise reward. Have no hidden desire. Recognize your spiritual objectives not self-centered but pleasing God. In fasting you have to put disciplinary measures to yield obedience in your fasting in order to have control. Whatever spiritual operation you undertake, the first thing to do is to fast. Do not forget whilst fasting to take bath often with consecrated water (pray on the water and the soap) or herbalated water (hyssop, sage, mint, basil etc.), and anoint your body Matt. 6:16-18, this will attract the angelic host, Angels are allies in collaboration, given by the Holy Spirit, in order to achieve a successful mission. Elijah was fed by an angel of God. They have God's name in them. Before undertaking any spiritual activities or operation, unless you have been instructed you should fast for three days and set your mind on the desired intention with prayers, mourning afternoon and evening.

Conclusion: The constant practice of fasting and prayers will draw you closer to the omnipotent and nothing will be hidden from you. A good and pleasing fasting before God will also help you bridge the gap between the higher consciousness and the brain level to achieve telepathic conveyance and receptive mind or spirit of discernment. Continuous fasting and prayer will attract an angelic corporate partner, which is the controller of the nine gifts. All things will be exposed to you, either interpretation of dreams, miracles, healing, protection, learning, fortune, prosperity and breakthrough, Good health, Righteousness, Glory to the Lord, Answered prayer, Refreshing, Continual guidance, Satisfaction, Restoration, work of endurance. All these is achieved with a God ordained fasting. No hindrance will stand your way.

THE PROMISE LAND

The Old Testament Promise land

In the old testament, the promise land was known as CANAAN. Abraham's father was mandated to go to Canaan but unfortunately died in the process of his journey to Canaan in HARAN. Genesis 11:31-32. Abraham's father Terah believed in God but represented God with objects, and did not know he was practicing idolatry. He did not give his heart completely to God unknowingly, but was religious and godly than the rest of the people. His improvised and partial friendly with God became the true worship of God at that time and paved way for the promised land. Why the promise land? Because God wanted to separate Terah and his descendants from the rest of the sinful world at that time so they can commit themselves as a nation to God. Ur was the place of conception of the mission of Canaan to Terah in the city of Chaldeans, meaning Ur was where Abraham's father lived before the revelation of Canaan was revealed and assigned to him. Chaldea was known as Mesopotamia, it joins Armenia and Euphrates. It was a land where more wheat was produced. This was the ancient name of Persia being southern part of Babylonia. Canaan was known as low land situated at the west of the Jordan and the Red Sea and between these waters and Mediterranean was given by God to Abraham and his descendants, the children of Israel. After the death of Abraham's father, Abram was frustrated. But his relationship with God was very strong, He believed in God, trusted God and sought His presence always, Abraham saw the mistake of his father and corrected that mistake by serving God without objects and this was the result of the continuation of the mission resulting in Gen. 12:4-5. Now the Lord had said to Abraham "Get out of your country, from your family and from your father's house to a land that I will show you. I will make you a great nation; I will bless you And make your name great; And you shall be a blessing. I will bless those who bless you And I will curse him who curse you. And in you, all the families of the earth shall be blessed." The bible says, Abraham departed as the Lord had commanded him to take everything and follow Him to the promise land which was mandated to his father, Terah. And Abraham was seventy-five years old when he departed from Haran Then Abraham took Sarah his wife and Lot his brother's son, and all their possessions that they had gathered and the people whom they had acquired in Haran and they departed to go to the land of Canaan. So they came to the land of Canaan." Abraham obeyed God and believed whatever God told him to be true and acted, left his country and departed as God said. God blessed Abraham as He promised. The bible says Abraham was very rich in Cattle, in Silver and in Gold. Abraham never stopped remembering God, wherever he went, he called on His name. Gen. 13:1-4. After the conflict with Lot he finally came to the land of Canaan. Isaac was born in the land of Canaan, Sarah, Isaac's mother and Abraham's wife died in Canaan Gen. 23:2. Sarah was buried at Canaan Gen 23:19. Abraham lived and died in Canaan and was buried at Canaan near his wife Sarah Gen 25:10. This means God fulfilled His promise by bringing Abraham to the promise land. So Abraham brought the Hebrews to the promise land as God's people. Hebrew was the ancient name of Israel. But the twelve tribe rebelled against God by rejecting the revelation God gave to Joseph and plotted to kill him. Even the father whose name is Jacob rejected the revelation. And God has to glorify Himself somewhere else. For them to know that Joseph's anointing on him was from God, and that revelation has to come to pass, so God was glorify in Egypt instead of Canaan - Israel. God said, the whole Israel, Jacob himself, the wife Rebecca, and the twelve tribe will bow before Joseph as the dream said so for rebellion they were damned to slavery and remained in Egypt. And as time went by they became and remained slaves which made them begin to cry unto God. And God who abide by His promise has to intervene by the hand of Moses back to the promised land. The creator did not stop creating human beings either bond or free for His glory, therefore He desired to save all and that led to the advent of Jesus Christ, His prophecy, His birth, His life and works on earth, His crucifixion, His resurrection back with the disciples, His ascension and His deity, resulting in the final completion of salvation not to Jews only but the world as whole.

New Testament Promise Land

Christ has appointed unto us a kingdom, where all the Christians will be led by Christ to the promise land of Heaven and this is the new testament Promise Land. The new testament promise land is different from the old testament promise land, in that about the old testament promise land, the people new where they were going but did not know how to get there, but the Christ promised land is more complex and difficult for one to believe and explain, which means the Christian faith is more stronger than the Hebrews faith to the promise land for (1) the Christians do not know where that promise land is located but (2) know how to get there and how it's going to come. If our hope, the Lord and our savior Christ Jesus fails to come back then all the Christians have failed and misled and are in terrible trouble. But we trust in Him because He is God the Son. And God does not lie. As Christians we strongly have that faith and cannot be disputed. Some people had gone there and are still there, Enoch, Elijah and Jesus Himself and Jesus took the disciples to the mountain and transfigured and show them those people with Him, Enoch as Moses and Elijah. As Enoch and Elijah continue with Him so Jesus urges Christians to continue with Him. Luke 22:28-30. "But you are those who have continued with Me in my trials. And I appoint upon you a kingdom as My Father had appointed unto Me. That you may eat and drink at My table in My kingdom and sit on thrones judging the twelve tribes of Israel." Even when we do not have His physical presence, we continue with Him till He comes back.

We have the faith that He will come back, which Christians are having super faith beyond the faith of Abraham, believing to receive what does not exist, a destination very difficult to describe and not easy for any ordinary Christian or person to believe. A believe, some may call it craziness. Abraham knew where he was going, he knew Canaan existed and where it was situated but heaven who can tell where it could be found but we believe and trust God to be there for us, a destination we are yet to reach. Jesus is the Lamb and the church is the bride and so Jesus says those who will continue in this call will share with Him the marriage supper celebration, Quote "Rev. 19:9. Blessed are they which are called into the marriage supper of the Lamb."

Jesus has promised Christians that He is going to prepare the promised Land and come back to take those who will wait John 14:1-3. "Let not your heart be troubled; you believe in God, believe also in Me. In My Father's house are many mansions; if it were not so I would have told you. I go to prepare a place for you. And if I go and prepare a place for you, I will come again and receive you unto Myself; that where I am, there you may be also." He had even promised us that whatever Christians had left behind and followed Him will not be wasted but they will receive hundred fold in this period of salvation on earth and in heaven. Matt. 19:28-30. In 2Peter 3:13. "Nevertheless we according to His promise look for new Heaven and a new Earth where in dwells righteousness." So the place Our Lord and Savior Jesus Christ is preparing, is the new heaven and the new earth meant for those who will patiently wait for His second coming.

Jesus said in John 3:11-12 "Most assuredly, I say to you We speak what We know and testify what We have seen and you do not receive Our witness. If I told you earthly things and you do not believe, how will you believe if I tell you heavenly things."

We have to consider that things of the old testament are physical and that of the new testament are more of the spiritual realm. Eg. The old testament baptism was the circumcision of the foreskin but the new testament circumcision has nothing to do with the foreskin but the receiving of the Holy Spirit or Holy Ghost baptism. If right now you will repented and accepted the Lord Jesus as your Lord and Savior, you will be saved and will be part of the mission to heaven. Because by grace we are saved through faith in Jesus Christ which is gift of God and not ourselves.

TITHE

John 1:1 In the beginning was the word and the word was with God and the word was God. God worked with the word and the word is the bible. With HIM- the word, God speaks to us, God is our spiritual father, so if we neglect what the bible say, we become rebellious to God and our relationship with HIM, Lord Jesus.

MEMORY VERSE: Malachi. 3:8." Will a man rob God? Yet ye have rob me. But ye say, wherein have we robbed thee? In Tithe and offering."

Purpose:

1. Provide for the work of God.
2. Prove believer's faithfulness
3. Pay honor to God
4. To feed the widow and the fatherless
5. Care for the priest (pastor, evangelist, prophets etc.).

MEANING:

Tithe is a covenant or agreement between God and his children. It is the tenth part of your earnings as children of God dedicated to the house of God. Therefore every child of God is oblige to pay tithe. Tithe is a contribution God is more particular with. Tithe is for people with faith you can't pay tithe if you have no faith in God. We are fortunate to be asked to pay tithe as Christians. Tithe identifies you as the child of God. God did not give tithe to Muslims, nor Buddhist or fetish priest but to his children, as an identification, so that God can bless them. So as tithe participant you are special. The gift of the Holy Spirit depend upon your tithe and righteousness as tithe displays the faithfulness of the tither. **(Gen. 14:19-20, Heb. 7:1-6, Rom. 4:3,21-25).**

REASON

Gen. 1:1. The bible says, In the beginning God created the heaven and earth." He did not mix any chemicals to create the earth, he did not mix medicines or herbs together to create the earth but: "By the word He created the earth. **Gen. 1:11.** And God said, let the earth bring forth grass, the herb that yield seed and fruit-tree that yields fruit according to its kind, whose seed is in itself, on the earth, and it was so. We know that, this comprises also of the minerals like, gold, silver, iron ore, coal etc. **Gen. 2:5-7.** And every plant of the field and minerals before it was in the earth, because God has not rain upon the earth because there was not a man to work on the ground. But there went up a mist from the earth and watered the whole face of the ground. And the Lord God formed man of the dust of the ground and breathed into his nostrils the breath of life and man became a living soul. Now the rain had expose the gold, diamond, silver, bauxite, manganese, iron ore jasper, sapphire jacinth, amethyst, chrysoprasus, chrysolyte topaz and saduins. **Gen. 1:21.** God created every living creature that moveth, sheep, goats, cows, bull houses, fouls and the great and small creatures of the sea and creatures of the air. **Gen. 1:27-28.** God created man and blessed man with wisdom and power to do wonderful things: planes, cars, ships, radio waves etc with materials God has put into the earth. The wisdom to make big factories to make money. And after making money we are entitled to pay tithe to God (that's to the church – for the work of God) but we for get about Him. So God spoke in. **Malachi. 3:8.** "Will a man rob God, Yet you have robbed Me But you say, In what way have we robbed You? In tithes and offerings. **Job 38:4.** "Where were you when I laid the foundation of the earth. Tell Me if you have understanding." **Malachi 3:9-12.** "You are cursed with a curse, for you have robbed Me, even this whole nation. Bring all the tithes into the storehouse, And try Me now in this, says the Lord of Host. If I will not open you the windows of heaven and pour out for you such blessing that there will not be room enough to receive it. And I will rebuke the devourer for your sake, so that he will not destroy the fruit of you ground, nor shall the vine fail to bear fruit for you in the field, says the Lord of Host; and all nations will call you blessed, For you will be a delightful land says the Lord of host."

Alfred Awortwe - Adams

The Lord is asking us to pay tithe (rent) on the earth we occupy, materials and all that we take. Some say when JESUS CAME He did not speak of tithe so tithe is not necessary but Jesus spoke in proverbs and even the disciples questioned Him why He always spoke in parables. This is what Our Lord Jesus Christ said about tithe: **Quote Matt. 21:33-40.** Hear another parable: "There was a certain landowner who planted a vineyard and set a hedge around it, dug a vine press in it and built a tower. And he leased it to vinedressers, and went into a far country. Now when winetage-time drew near, he sent his servants to the vinedresser that they might receive it's fruit. And the vinedressers took his servants beat one, killed one and stoned another. Again he sent other servants more than the first, and they did likewise to them. Then last of all, he sent his son to them, saying they will respect my son. But when the vinedressers saw the son, they said among themselves, this is the heir, come let us kill him and seize his inheritance. So they took him and cast him out of the vineyard and killed him. Therefore, when the owner of the vineyard comes, what will he do to the vinedressers? **Verse 41** they answered, he will destroy those wicked men miserably, and lease his vineyard to other vinedressers who will render to him the fruits in their seasons". He also said in **Matt. 23:23.** "Woe to you Scribes and Pharisees, hypocrites! For you pay tithe of mint and anise and cumin and have neglected the weightier matters of the law: justice and mercy and faith. These you ought to have done, **without leaving the others undone."** Jesus said without leaving the commandment of tithe and all the laws of Moses, meaning He said, we have to pay tithe.

And again, all that Jesus is saying is that, The Father is asking mankind to pay tithe because that's the rent of the World we live in. God is saying I have given you the world (the earth) to live in and do every business you want even the things in and on the earth as material for your business but at the end of the month or the year you should bring me one-tenth of whatever you made as long as you live in the world. Jesus has confirmed the offering of tithe to the church, for the church represent the house of God, the storehouse of God. At the end of the month we quickly have to pay our rent of our habitation, even if we do not have the means we do everything possible so that we are not thrown out. But that house is in the world (on earth), as the landlord will throw the tenant out when he fails to pay his rent even so God will throw our houses out of the face of the earth with an earthquake, tornado, hurricane or volcano. We cherish to fear human being more than the creator. Even if our landlords throws us out, we are still living and do every business we like on the earth. But we honor the landlord more than our creator. When we fail to pay our tithe, we become enemies of God, what did David say: **1Samuel 25:21-22.** "Now David had said, Surely in vain I have protected all that this fellow has in the wilderness, so that nothing was missed of all that belongs to him. And he has repaid me with evil for good. May God do so and more also to the enemies of David if I leave one male of all who belong to him by morning light." When we fail to pay our tithe, we become enemies to God, exactly like Nabal and his house became enemies to David.

FUNCTION

In Malachi 3:1. Bring all the tithe into the storehouse and it's where the treasuries of the dedicated things and the treasuries of the house of God are brought, as said in **1Chron. 26:20**. So it is sin not to pay tithe. And also incorrect payment of tithe is also sin and can lead to curse. The very day God placed you in your mother's womb that He made this covenant with you, so it's a violation as able human being not to pay tithe. **Deut. 8:11-12; 17-18**. "Beware that you do not forget the Lord your God by not keeping His commandments, His judgments, and His statues which I command you today, lest when you have eaten and are full and have built beautiful houses and dwell in them". **Verse 17-78** "then you say in your heart, my power and the might of my hand have gained me this wealth. But you shall remember the Lord your God for it is He who gives you power to get wealth that He may establish His covenant which He swore to your fathers as it is this day." It is God the father, the father of our Lord Jesus Christ who supplies you power, strength and knowledge to acquire the wealth you possess, therefore you need to honor him with your wealth to pay tithe of ten percent unto your God.

BENEFIT:- Malachi. 3:8-10. God has talked to us cordially to bring the tithe on the things we take from Him, God is a living God and promise us abundant blessing. He has promised us protection and great popularity. He also promised us protection which is the HEDGE: Job 1:10. If you refuse to pay tithe, you loose the hedge (that's the fire of the Holy Spirit) God has set around you. So brothers and sisters try to pay your tithe to identify yourself as a child of God, the seed of Abraham and the heir of God. Proverbs. 3:9-10. "Honor the Lord with thy first fruit and your barns shall be filled with plenty."

EXTRACTS:- Hebr. 7:8-9 Exo. 16:36 Gen. 14:22-29; Gen. 28:20-22 1Cor. 16:1-2 Num. 18:21-28 Matt. 22:21;Matt. 23:23 Deut. 14:22-28; Deut. 8:18 Malachi. 1:7-8 Nehemiah 10:35-58

Deut. 26:12-13." When thou hast made an end of good tithing, all the tithes of thine increase of the third year which is the year of tithing, and hast given it unto the Levite, the stranger, the fatherless, and the widow, that they may eat within thy gates, and be filled. Thou shall say before the Lord thy God, I have brought away the hallowed things out of mine house, and also have given them unto the Levite, and unto the stranger, to the fatherless, and to the widow, according to all thy commandments which thou hast commanded me: I have not transgress thy commandments, neither have I forgotten them. I have not eaten any of it when in mourning, nor have I removed any of it for an unclean use, nor given any of it for the dead. I have obeyed the voice of the Lord my God, and have done according to all that You have commanded me. **Look down from Your holy habitation, from heaven and bless Your people Israel and the land which You have given us, just as You swore to our fathers, a land flowing with milk and honey."** This is a covenant and once you honor your part God is committed, He cannot get out of this covenant till He also honor His part. For it's His own words from His tongue through His lips. In Malachi. 3:10 -12, He has stated exactly what He will do in your life if you pay your tithe correctly and your offering.

Lev. 27:31-34 "And if a man will at all redeem ought of his tithes, he shall add thereto the fifth part thereof. All the tithe of the herd, or of the flock, even of whatsoever pass under the rod, the tenth shall be holy unto the Lord. He shall not search whether it be good or bad, neither shall he change it and if he change it at all, then both it and the change thereof shall be holy: it shall not be redeemed." Because tithe is a covenant, God has place strict measures on it and must be obeyed.

1Cor. 9:13-14 Do ye not know that they which minister about holy things live of the things of the temple? And they which wait at the altar are partakers of the altar? Even so hath the Lord ordained that they which preach the gospel should live of the gospel.

HEAVEN
(YOUR NEXT DESTINATION)

Heaven is a vast universe beyond description. It is the great universe, whose advancement is infinite. **It is about infinity in area and cannot be compared to just a universe**. It is a place God has prepared unto those who love him and believe in Christ.

John 14:1 Let not your heart be troubled. ye believe in God, believe also in me.

Because, that God you believe is the one standing with you. Jesus Christ is God, if he is not God, he wouldn't have commanded the wind to humble itself before him, and the wind obeyed. If he is not God he wouldn't have asked the hurricane to be obedient before him, and the sea obeyed. If he is not God he wouldn't have asked death to come out of Lazarus who had died four days and buried, and death, Satan's greatest weapon against humanity obeyed and came out of Lazarus and Lazarus lived, He Is The Living God. The scripture says in the beginning the spirit of God was moving upon the face of the waters and He came to the physical realm and walked physically on the water. If he is not God, the sea would not have obeyed and hold him in suspense on the surface of the water. He is God, in Hebrews 1: 5-8. For which of the angels did He ever say; You are my Son, Today I have gotten You? And again I will be to Him a Father and He shall be to Me a Son? But when He again brings the first fruit to the world, He says; Let all the angels of God worship Him. And of the angels, He says: Who make His angels spirits And His ministers a flaming fire/ But to the Son, He says: YOUR THRONE, O GOD, IS FOREVER AND EVER; A SCEPTER OF RIGHTEOUSNESS IS THE SCEPTER OF YOUR KINGDOM (Ps.45:6-7

John 13:19. Now I tell you before it comes that when it comes to pass ye may believe that I am "He."

You have to believe now not when it has come to pass, it will be late, when Jesus had already taken his throne for judgment, to tell Jesus now I believe. Thomas did not believe Jesus when he was told, Jesus has risen and lost the great blessing because Jesus blessed those who had not seen him and believed. The same applies to Heaven, people don't believe there is Heaven which the father had prepared through Jesus Christ for those who have faith in Christ, that's those who love God through Jesus. Anyone who does not believe in Christ, there is no life eternal for him, because only in Christ Jesus you can find eternal life therefore, there is no heaven for the Christ infidels. Without the Lord Jesus Christ we will not see the father. It's only by Jesus we will see the father.

Jesus said in John 14:2-3, 8-9. In my father's house are many mansions; if it were not so I would have told you. I go to prepare a place for you. And if I go to prepare a place for you, I will come again, and receive you unto myself; that where I am, there you may be also. Philip said unto him, Lord show us the father and it suffices us. Jesus said unto him, I have been so long with you and yet has thou not known me, Philip? He that hath seen me hath seen the father: and how saith thou then, show us the father?" So in Jesus is the father, in Jesus is the Holy Ghost, in Jesus is the Godhead bodily found. That is the hope of a Christian. All Christians have this in mind. **Two thousand years and over** since Jesus left, he has not finished the place he was going to prepare for his followers, how complex and beautiful the place is. We cannot compare the earth to the beauty in heaven. This project is almost completed, it's only left with the finishing touches. Very soon Christ will come with the reward for those who served him according to his WILL. Brother if you have not taken Christ, look for a Christ church and go to accept Christ so that you don't regret, that you will have a place in God when Jesus Christ returns with his reward.

Hebrews 11:16. "But now they desire a better country, that is, an heavenly: wherefore God is not ashamed to be called their God.: for he had prepared for them a city." God is pleased to call us His people and to us our God, we lost this grace but by the love of God and the grace of our Lord Jesus Christ we have been restored and today we can be proud to be called God's people. Eph. 2:19. Now, therefore, you are no longer strangers and foreigners, but fellow citizens with the saints and members of the household of God - meaning we were born under a an unknown kingdom but after accepting Christ we are reborn and no more strangers and foreigners in the kingdom of God. We were but now no.

Hosea 11:9 For I am GOD and not MAN. The HOLY ONE in the mist of thee.

The holy one means whatever He had said He is able to do. Something no man can do. He has promise us heaven, He will surely do, it's a wonderful paradise. The things that are impossible with man are possible with God. There are every evidence and instances in the bible that prove that this Heaven exist.

DECRIPTION OF HEAVEN

Rev. 21:16 And the city lieth four square, and the breadth is as long as the length: And he measured the city with the reed, twelve thousand heavenly furlongs. The length and the breadth and the height of it are equal. **21:17**. And he measure the wall thereof, an hundred and forty and four cubits, according to the measure of a man, that is, of the angel.

A normal human form in heaven is beyond description as compared to earthly human beings. The bible says the angels which deserted their habitation who were the sons of God saw the daughters of men that they were fair and they took them wives of all which they chose and bare them children which were giants and mighty men, in that they were also become flesh, because they became human, they were stripped off their heavenly appearance, and even the little heavenly energy left in them the bible says they were giants.

So you can see how fearful Angels can be, left alone the **TRINITY**. As soon as angels are sent to the earth they take the normal earthly human form, they transfigure Matt. 17:2-8. **1Kings 8:27**. "But will God indeed dwell on the earth? Behold the Heaven and Heaven of Heavens cannot contain thee; How much less this house that I have built? Yet have thou respect unto the prayer of thy servant and to his supplication, O Lord my

God to hearken unto the cry and to the prayer which thy servant prays before thee today". So one furlong in heaven is thousand and thousand by thousand furlongs on earth. The bible says, one day is with the Lord as thousand years and a thousand years as one day. **2 Pet. 3:8.** What we have to understand is thousand years on the earth is one day in heaven and one day in heaven is three hundred and sixty-five thousand earthly days. So your boastful hundred years on earth is just two and half hours in heaven.

When we look at the mosquito its longest lifespan is three to four or five days, but the mosquito knows it has lived long a lifespan on earth. Even so our heavenly two and half hours seemed too long for us on the earth. James 4:14 Whereas ye know not what shall be on the morrow, for what is your life? It is even a vapor, that appears for a little time, then vanishes away. So you could see we are just little passing being before the angels. But the angels are compare to love us because the father which is the creator loves us.

Rev. 21:18. And the buildings of the wall of it was of jasper, and the city was pure gold, like unto clear glass. Jasper is one of the wonderful precious stones with very high world demand, more difficult to come by, you can imagine the cost of an ounce of this stone, more precious than gold. It is this mineral which is used in the construction of houses in heaven. Gold in heaven is just a common stone. The whole roads and streets in heaven is made of gold and the ground also made of gold. As we do not value the soil of the earth we walk on it, we urine on it and do all sort of filthy things on it, so gold is very common, the heavenly beings look on and walk on it. If gold of a size like the football is released from heaven to New York City downtown-Manhattan or in the Bronx or downtown Brooklyn, millions of people will suffer death from the gun and will belonged to no body, whilst in heaven people walk over it. That which the dog will see and bark the cat will close its eyes, it's nothing for the cat. So the Christian is glorified.

Rev. 21:19-20 And the foundations of the wall of the city were garnished with all manner of precious stones, The first foundation was jasper; the second sapphire; the third chalcedony; the fourth an emerald; the fifth sardonyx; the sixth sardius; the seventh chrysolyte; the eight beryl; the ninth topaz; the tenth chrysoprasus; the eleventh a jacinth; the twelfth an amethyst. This is describing the procedure of construction in heaven. The buildings have twelve stages of foundation, each step of the foundation is made of different material, unshakable and untouchable, so one can imagine how strong the buildings will be. These stones are precious stone mixed with the gold for the foundations of the buildings in heaven and the whole wall of the twelve cities. The area of the city is of indefinite measure to the area of the universe. The timber in heaven is diamond. The furniture is of diamond. The whole ground of heaven is gold. The foundation of the buildings being excavated is gold. Gold has no value to the people of heaven, it's value is only on the earth. From the time of Adam we have not been able to finish developing the earth, Only small part of the earth is developed which is less than half the area of the earth, and to completely develop the earth will take another twelve thousand years, that's from Adam to present [that's Adam to Noah to Abraham to Moses to David to Jesus to Obama, every 2000 years God sends someone for such identical purpose but Jesus' was superior to all, demonstrating His deity. How then do we expect Jesus to finish that great work of heaven which He promised in John 14, which is over ten times the universe in two thousand years but He is God. Christ is doing something extraordinary for Christians. God is not man therefore God does not do what man can do, and this makes Him God. I hope every body will have the desire to be there, and Christians will have the patience and waiting spirit from God. It's a fantastic and awesome place. People still doubt the existence of Heaven but there are some people who have been taken to heaven and they are still there, they have not return to the earth. Enoch, was taken to heaven Gen. 5:24, Elijah was taken to heaven 2Kings 2:11 and Jesus the son of God was taken to heaven Acts 1:9. As Moses was on the mountains, the Sinai and people complained he was not returning but finally he returned to the people so Jesus has tarry for too long, yet He will return to us. Jesus is doing a great work and is going to take extra more years. But those who will continue to wait on Him will be saved. Heaven is a great place, our ultimate destination, please have the desire to be there and you will never regret. You will see that this earth is not a place for you but no human being can go to heaven without passing through this earth, that's not possible.

This is heaven, is the hope of a Christian. But you who is not a Christian, what is your hope, the Christian has another hope also in the grave. In

Matt. 28:20 Christ said "I am with you always even unto the end of the world." Even when the Christian is dead, so far as the world has not come to the end, the judgment day has not yet come, the Holy Spirit, the angels of God, all are with the Christian even in the grave till the end comes. For this promise to be yours, if you have not receive Christ Jesus as your Lord and savior, do so now. When Lazarus was dead and laid in the tomb [John 11], Jesus commanded him to come out, and Jesus commanded the people to loose him which means Lazarus was bound with linen according to the culture of the Israelites [John 11:44]. How was he able to come and stand at the gate of the tomb? This shows that there were angels with him in the tomb who brought him to the gate by the command of Jesus. And the people loosed him and came to live again among the living. Likewise you will also have angels with you in your grave and you will never be alone. Do not wait till tomorrow for tomorrow may not be for you. Just lift up your hands and read this prayer below loudly.

Thank you father God, for your wonderful love towards me. Even though I rebelled against you and took to my own way, you did not abandoned me but took good care of me, I am still alive. Thank you for your mighty power and mercy towards me. The bible says! "For God so love the world that he gave his only begotten son, that whosoever believes in him shall not perish, but have everlasting life." Father God you are the only TRUE HOLY LIVING GOD. I repent Lord, I repent. Lord Jesus, I do not know how to express my thanks to you: because you laid down your life for my sake and poured out your blood to purchase me, at a very expensive price. Father Lord Jesus, today I lift up my hands to receive you as my Lord and Savior. Forgive me all my sins and receive me unto yourself. Lord of host I thank you. I will worship you for the rest of my life. Thank you Holy Ghost for your touch and drawing me unto my Lord and savior Jesus Christ. Thank you Lord of the harvest, thank you my Lord. IN JESUS MIGHTY NAME. AMEN.

Today, as you have said this prayer, you belong to Christ and you have the right to receive the promise which Christ has promised unto Christians join a church. Have the desire to be baptized. God Bless you.

CHAPTER THREE

THE FRUIT OF LIFE

MEMORY VERSE:- Romans 10:14-15

TOPICE: WALKING IN THE SPIRIT, AND BEARING FRUIT (Gal. 5:16-26.)

Vs.16-This I say that walk in the spirit, and ye shall not fulfill the lust of the flesh.

Vs. 19-now the work of the flesh are manifest which are these.

THE FRUIT OF THE FLESH

The fruit of the flesh is the things that we do that does not glorify God. Things which lead us into sin. Once we are in the flesh we do not talk about things of God, but things that glorify us and exalt the devil. One may ask after all, what are the things of the flesh. Some of the things of the flesh are explain below.

Adultery: voluntary sexual intercourse between a married person and unmarried person or between different married couples. 1cor.3:16-17; Prov. 6:32-33; Lev.20:10;_Mark 10:11-12; 1Cor.6:16; Prov. 30:20

Fornication-: sexual activity between unmarried persons. Deut.22:23-24,28-29;Heb.13:4; 1Cor. 6:16;Cor.7:1-2; Prov. 31:3;

Lasciviousness: action or feeling expressing and influencing sexual desire, that's lust. Prov.23:33; Col. 4:6;2Tim2:16

Idolatry: the worship of idol, too much devotion or admiration to idols, materialism and paganism. Eze. 8:9-16; Exo. 32:2-4.

Variance: having difference of opinion or disagree. (in conflict). Deviate.

Sedition: word or action intended to make people rebel against the authority of the state (Brain wash),(undermining) or leadership of a religious body. Acts 13:6-12

Hatred: very strong dislike, animosity, prejudice or hostility.

Witchcraft: The use of evil powers. Lev. 19:31; Lev. 20:6,27;Exo. 22:18;2 Sam.21:6 2King 6:28-29; Acts 19:13-17.

Uncleanness: Spiritually impure, lack of spiritual purity. Being talkative is a sin, talking against a brother, against your pastor, staying on the phone for hours with vain talk inquisitiveness and insinuations and talking bitterly behind brother, all these are uncleanness, evil and sinful. Prov. 16:25; Lev.21:12; Lev. 19:12; Eph. 4:31; Prov. 13:31;

Wrath: extreme anger. Prov. 16:14.

Strife: violence disagreement, state of conflict. 1Sam. 19:1.Eze. 8:17-18; Hosea 4:4;

Heresies: Opinion that is contrary to what is generally accepted. eg. religion. 1 John 4:1-3; Mark 9:38-40; 1 Cor. 10:27-28; Matt. 7:15-23.

Envy: Feeling of discontent and bitterness 1Sam.18:28-29: Mark 15:10

Murder: Unlawful killing of human being intentionally. Matt. 5:21; Exo.20:13;2Sam.12:9.

Reveling.: Making merry, noisy celebration, Being much interested in ungodly things; reveling until dawn. Prov. 21:17a.

Emulation: competitive action - trying to be better than the others or effort to excel over others or prideful look, eg if I am not there nobody can do it. Prov. 6:17; 16:18

Drunkenness the habit of excessive use of alcohol. Gen.9:20-24; Gen.19:30-38; Prov.23:3132,21, Prov. 31:3-6; Prov. 20:1; Prov.5:11-12,22; Joel 1:5;Hab. 2:15; Prov.21:17b; Dan.1:8; Rom. 13:13; Eph. 5:18;

And Such Like: Smoking, Pride, 1Cor. 3:16-17; Lev. 19:11,13; Prov. 16:1-Prov. 16:18; Job 41:20; Laziness: Prov. 19:15,24; 20:4,13; 6:9-11; 22:13; 18:9; 6:4-12; 21:25;12:27; Defrauding: Prov. 22:22; 28:3; 29:13, Stealing: Exo. 20:5, Lev. 19:11, Josh.7:19-25, Eph. 4:28

THE FRUIT OF THE SPIRIT

Goodness: The quality of being kind, quality that nourishes growth, favorable character, praise worthy character, fertile, Acts 10:38; Matt. 14:14; Col. 3:14; Gal. 6:9-10, Heb. 13:16; Eph. 6:8-9; Prov. 28:27; Prov. 19:17; Deut. 15:7-8;

Temperance: Calmness of the mind, composure, self restrain in one's behavior, moderation (control in behavior, self control). 1Pet. 1:6, Gal. 5:23, Acts 24:25.

Faith: Trusting in the invisible to be visible, strong believe, believe and trust in God and loyalty to God. Firm believe in something for which there is no Proof (trust is the main icon of faith), Unquestionable confidence. Heb. 11:1-6; Rom. 1:17; Rom. 10:17;

Love: Helping others; Putting ones life at stake for others; Helping to make the church what it is supposed to be, and to put new life into people. 1Cor. 13:4-8; 1John 3:16; Rom. 5:8; 1John 4:10; Matt. 22:36-40 (Deut. 6:4-7; Prov. 17:17; Heb. 13:1,3; Deut. 7:9 (Exo. 20:6); Matt. 5:8.

Joy: Feeling of great happiness, the emotion expressed by well - being, success, good fortune, the prospect of possessing what one desire. The joy of a Christian is to do the will of God and be blessed, and when we refuse to do the will of God we loose the joy in Christ. James 4:6; John 15:11; Acts 20:24; Matt. 25:21;

Peace: The state of violence free from within and outside, absolute security and externally from oppressive thoughts, emotions and actions. John 14:27; Col 3:5.

Meekness: Humbleness, Obedience, gentleness, submission, having no resentment (ill-feeling). Mark 7:25-30; Matt. 5:5; 11:29;

Forgiveness: Allowing room to completely forget an error. 2Cor. 2:10-11; Matt. 6:14-15; Matt.18:15-17; 2Cor. 6:15-18; Matt. 18:21-35; Rom. 16:20; Matt.5:9; Lev. 19:18; Gal.6:1-10; 2Cor. 2:10-11; Gal. 5:25-26; 2Cor. 5:14-19;Luk.15:20; Matt.18:23-35; Matt. 5:39-48;

With these we know what to do and what not to do. Which things may lead us to be sinners and which good lifestyle we must lead as Christians.

FORGIVENESS OF SIN: AND HOW IT WORKS. TO ATTRACT FAVOR

MEMORY VERSE:

2Corinthians 2:10-11. Now whom you forgive anything I also forgive, for if indeed I have forgiven anything, I have forgiven that one for your sake in the presence of Christ. Lest Satan should take advantage of us for we are not ignorant of his devices. (the greatest device of Satan is unforgiveness).

2Corinthians 5:17. Therefore if anyone be in Christ, he is a new creature, old things are passed away, behold, all things have become new.

MEANING: To completely forget someone's fault against us or to give up resentment (bitterness), Forgiveness is not by wisdom or power or knowledge of man, but of the mercy of God when we are broken in heart to walk with God.

THE LOVE OF GOD: God sacrificed the most expensive treasure in His custody, His Only Begotten Son Our Lord Jesus Christ to cleanse us of the grievous sin in the life of man, which brought condemnation to man. John 3:16-18. When we became His followers, we have been cleanse by faith, the old character and deeds is cancelled, we have started a new life, All sin is forgiven.

POWER OF CONFESSION: There has been no other way that man has received forgiveness of sin, other than repentance of sin and confession of sin. Roman 10:9-10, 2Corinthians 5:21.

TOTAL FORGIVENESS: We are totally forgiven when we have change of mind, repent and confess, and receive Jesus Christ as the Son of God and our Savior. 1John 1:9. This makes God to forget that we have ever sinned. Our godly memory is restored to us, condemnation is totally removed from us. Repentance and confession is the greatest weapon that draws God back to us and closes the gap between God and Man. It is the weapon which Satan hates and cannot withstand it.

TWO KINDS OF FORGIVENESS: (1). Godly forgiveness (2) Human forgiveness.

God expect us to forgive so that He could also forgive us. Matt. 6:14 For if you forgive men their trespasses your heavenly Father will also forgive you. But if you do not forgive men their trespasses neither will your Father in heaven forgive your trespasses. (Matt. 6:12).

After we have forgiven the trespasses of others against us, then the heart and body has been prepared to receive forgiveness from God. It is obvious that our heavenly Father will forgive us our sins. Most of the sayings and activities of the gospel are spiritual and until you believe, you will not understand.

Peter was eager to serve the Lord with open heart and tried to know from Jesus where he will stand in forgiveness to others. Matt. 18:21-22 Then Peter came to Him and said, Lord how often shall my brother sin against me and I forgive him? Up to seven times? Jesus said to him, I do not say to you up to seven times, but up to seventy times seven. Peter was convinced, Jesus said this, because the jews hardly forgive, they usually like to revenge and it was the other of that time, that once you revenge, that person stops coming after you and this was according to the order of Moses. Exodus 21:24. eye for eye and tooth for tooth. But this resulted in a very serious and horrible violence and there was no peace among them, eg. Genesis 34:25-29. The sons of Jacob destroyed the city of Shechem when the son of Hamor raped Dinah the daughter of Leah and Jacob. They never forgive even when the king said his son will marry Dinah and was prepared to give all that they will request, and killed all the people in the city and took their properties and assets for the sake of Dinah. Hebrew 10:30-31, 26. As Christians we have to seek for settlement and not confusion and violence. Jesus is telling us to do the possible best to we can to forgive and live in peace which will create a peaceful world environment and image. God does not live in violence environment and hate human violence.

Matt. 18:15-17 Moreover if your brother sin against you go and tell him his fault between you and him alone, if he hears you, you have gain your brother. But if he will not hear you take with you one or two more, that by the mouth of two or three witnesses every word may be established. And if he refuse to hear them, tell it to the church, but if he refuses even to hear the church, let him be to you a heathen and a tax collector.

Tax collector have no mercy, no matter how much small one owes, they will levi your property to pay exactly the amount, meanwhile they are the worse cheats and embezzlers.

Matt. 18:23-35 The parable of the unmerciful servant whom his Lord spared because he did not have the ability to pay his master what he owed him, but he was so wicked that his friend, a servant like him owed him very small amount which he demanded payment and his friend was not able and threw him in prison. When their Lord heard of his action, he called him back, threw him also and his family into an everlasting prison because there was no way for him to pay what he owed.

When Jesus asked for forgiveness of sin for the world, Luke 23:34 Then said Jesus, father forgive them: for they know not what they do. God began to pour all the sins of the world upon Jesus (extracted from the world). And because Jesus was holy in the flesh and in the spirit, the sins poured upon him became very heavy upon him and could not enter into his spirit, **(when sin enter into the spirit it becomes a curse and make one die in the spirit and continue to torment the person till this curse is broken and the person is delivered and set free.).** Mark 15:34 And at the ninth hour Jesus cried with a loud voice, saying, Eloi, Eloi, lama sa-bachthani? Which is being interpreted, My God, My God why hast thou forsaken me. and John 19:28. After this Jesus knowing that all things were now accomplished, that the scripture mighty be fulfilled, said, I thirst. His righteous spirit began to increase in strength and power and burnt off the sins poured upon him, John19:30. When Jesus therefore had received the vinegar, he said, It is finished: and he bow his head and gave up the ghost. After the sins were burnt Jesus then collected the sins and carry them and buried them in the grave and came back to life, Col.2:13-15. And having spoiled principalities and powers, he made a shew of them openly, triumphing over them in it. Jesus drove away the strongman and his army and chained the strongman under the sea and his ministers in the mountains, Jude 6. And the angels which kept not their first estate, but left their own habitation, he had reserved in everlasting chains under darkness unto the judgment of the great day. So when we ask for forgiveness of sin, God by forgiving us our sins, extract the sins from the spirit to leave the spirit clean and righteous, he then pours the sins upon the flesh, which means we also have our part to play for the forgiveness of our sins, there is no easy attitude in the things of God. The fire of the righteous spirit given by Christ battles to burn the sins. The moment we sin again the fire of the righteous spirit of Christ is quenched and the sins enter back into the spirit and demons and evil spirits take advantage and we are conquered. John 8:11; She said, no man, Lord. And Jesus said unto her, Neither do I condemn thee: go, and sin no more. Matt.12:43-48. When the unclean spirit is gone out of a man, he walks through dry places, seeking rest and finding none. Then he said, I will return into my house (**if someone dwells at a place for a long time he dominates the place spiritually and physically**) from hence I came out: and when he is come, he findeth it empty, swept, and garnished. Then goes he and takes with himself seven other spirits more wicked than himself, and they enter in and dwell there: and the last state of that man is worse than the first. Even so shall it be also unto this wicked generation.

A paralyzed man was carried by friends through the roof in front of Jesus who received his healing instantly when his sins were forgiven him by Jesus. Mark 2:5.

We also need to repent and confess our sins to receive forgiveness. 1John 1:9 If we confess our sins, he is faithful and just to forgive us our sins and to cleanse us from all unrighteousness. Confessing our sins and being obedient attracts God's favor. One thing we have to understand is that favor is a behavior which gives a person an advantage even if it is unfair. Once you have been forgiven your sins, you can attract favor **and it comes by meekness.**

CONCLUSION: Forgiveness is so important to God that every book of the bible talks about it. Once you are saved by the sacrifice and the blood of Jesus, God desires you to be His home made image and not a mass product image. So God has said, even when we are casting in our offering and there we remember that we have something against another person or brother in faith we first have to go and make peace with him then we can come and cast our offering in the offering bowl else the offering is not acceptable Matt. 5:23-26.

Matt. 5:9 "Blessed are the peace makers for they shall be called the Sons of God." (your adversary will complain bitterly against you and cause your down fall and make sure that you be like him and both of you will fall into hell).

Deuteronomy 32:35. "Vengeance is mine and recompense, their foot shall slip in due time, for the day of their calamity is at hand, and the things to come hasten upon them."

So it is not for us to judge people who offend or sin against us. It is the Lord who has the power to judge the person. Luke 15:20-24 We also have to remember the prodigal son, his father did not rejected him but accepted him back in the family. The father forgave him like you and I, Jesus Christ has forgiven us all our sins, why do we not also forgive others. Even though the prodigal son was totally forgiven, his guilty conscience limited him of his liberty in the family and his control over the family properties and was afraid to certain measures in the house. Once we forgive others, their guilty conscience will limit their relationship. It's natural.

SIN

The word sin when abbreviated means

S = Severe I = Instruction N = Neglected

So from the abbreviation we derive the word REBELLION, which is translated to mean SIN, Rebellion means strictly neglect and resist instruction. Hence to sin means to rebel or neglect severe instruction. Adam and Eve were not the first persons to sin. It was the devil who first sinned with a sizeable percentage of the angelic host. Adam and Eve were caused to sin by the word they heard and believed, **that's how sin come about**. We inherited sin from Adam and Eve as well as they also inherited it from the Satan. It may have been contradicting if God must create sinful humans. We are created by God and are all children of God, but we are all not His people. Being God's people is different from being His children. The people of God obey Him and do His will but not all children obey Him. We become sinners from the very first time we sinned as matured humans, meaning we inherited the nature to sin. Therefore we are not born with sin but assumed the continuation to sin. A child is not imputed with his sin but an adult is. We therefore have the choice to refuse to sin. It is the choice of man to choose to sin or not. Sin also means corrupt, and corruption is not man's nature but an acquired situation by **a natural tendency** of negligence to sin. Corruption is the rotten state of a material or object and may mean that it was acquired which moved from a good state to a bad state. This is how sin look like. Sin was originally not part of human dignity or philosophy. Gen. !:26" Let us make man in our image in our likeness and let them have dominion over the fish of the sea, over the bird of the air, and over the cattle, over all the earth and over every creeping thing that creeps on earth." So the decision of God creating man was a perfect decision to create a perfect man who had no bleach or impediment Eccl. 7:29 "Truly this only have I found that God made man upright but they have sought out many schemes." The bible also says in Pvov. 14:12 "There is a way that seems right to a man but the end is the way of death". And it says also "because of these things, the wrath of God is coming upon the sons of disobedience." Gal. 3:6.

Hence, sin is the breaking of God's law or failure to obey the commandments of God. In otherwise it's the rejection of His commandments and God, and living a way contrarily to God's principle.

MEMORY VERSE:

1John 3:8 He who sin is of the devil, for the devil has sinned from the beginning. For this purpose the son of God was manifested that He might destroy the works of the devil.

There are two major sins in life.

1. THE REJECTION OF JESUS CHRIST
2. THE WORSHIP OF IDOLS

THE REJECTION OF JESUS CHRIST: From creation to date we know that Adam and his wife Eve made a horrible mistake which brought condemnation unto them which has affected the whole race of mankind. And God needed someone to intercede and there was none. Eze.22:30 "So I sought for a man among them who will make a wall and stand in the gap before Me on behalf of the land, that I should not destroy it; but I found none." So Christ who is the surety, the co-signer has to be delivered for that sacrifice for the remission of the sins of the world, unto salvation, as the bible says, Hebr. 7:22 "by so much more Jesus has become a surety of a better covenant":

THE TWO TREASURES OF CHRIST TO MANKIND:

1. The blood of Christ which has the power to cleans us, that's the remission of sin.
2. The body of Christ which has the power to save, that's has given us salvation.

This means without remission of sin there will be no salvation.

Heb. 9:22 "And according to the law almost all things are purified with blood, and without shedding of blood there is no remission." verse 20 And this is the blood of the covenant which God commanded you.

Hebr. 10:28-30, 31 "Anyone who has rejected Moses law dies without mercy on the testimony of two or three witnesses. Of how much worse punishment do you suppose, will he, be thought worthy who has trampled the Son of God under foot, counted the blood of the covenant by which he was sanctified a common thing and insulted the Spirit of grace (the Holy Spirit). It is a fearful thing to fall into the hands of the living God"

There is every proof and indication that Christ was made our appeasement, therefore it's a terrible sin to reject Him, confirmed by the following bible quotation.

John 6:29 It is the work of God that you believe in whom He sent.

John 6:38 Jesus came down from heaven to do the will of God.

John 6:46 No one has seen God except Jesus. Exo. 33:20.

John 6:51 Christ is the living bread from heaven, the bread is the fresh of Christ, those who eat will live forever.

John 6:44 No one can come to Christ unless God draws him.

John 6:40 The will of God is that those who see Christ and believe may have everlasting life and will be raised the last day.

John 8:56-58 Abraham rejoice when he saw Jesus. The Jews were confused and said you are not yet fifty years and you have seen Abraham. Jesus said before Abraham I was.

John 12:26 Where I am there My servants will be, if any serves Me him My Father will honor. Christ is ordained as the God of the world

Roman 5:8-10 God demonstrated His love towards us while we were sinners Christ died for us. God has the ability to save us through Christ.

1Cor. 6:19-20 Our bodies is the temple of the Holy Spirit. We are not our own. We are bought with a price

Hebr. 10:26 If we sin willfully now that we know the truth there remain no longer sacrifice for our sins.

Hebr. 10:14 By one sacrifice we are perfected for ever

Hebr. 9:28 Christ was offered once to bear the sins of many, those who wait will see Him, if they do not sin, for salvation.

1Pet. 2:24 He bore our sins in His body on the tree, by whose strips we are healed.

Gal. 3:13 Christ has redeemed us from the curse of the law haven become a curse for us for it is written CURSE IS EVERYONE WHO HANGS ON A TREE.

Eph. 2:14. Christ has broken the middle wall of separation.

So we have no excuse to reject Christ as our savior.

THE WORSHIP OF IDOLS:

After the advent of the sin of Adam and Eve, man was desperate for God and did not know where to begin and to end. Man knew there was God but cannot see God anymore. So man substituted God with objects and after time man's faith was diverted to those objects, which took man's faith in God. And this has been and till now, for some, idols has been their god. Psalm 106:35-40; Deut. 7:16; Lev. 17:7;

Exo. 32:1-10. God hates idolism and the main taboo in the house of God. Psalm 115:4-8 idols are motionless for they can not talk. Psalm 14:1-2 The fool says in his heart, there is no God.[Psalm 53:1]. Idol worship is the origin of all sin which has been the result in all mankind, inheriting a situation to sin and has led to many different kinds of sins. Gal. 4:8 "But then indeed when you did not know God you served those which by nature are not god's. Lev. 24:17 "Whoever kills any man shall surely be put to death". Lev. 19:31 "Give no regard to mediums and familiar spirits, do not seek after them, to be defile by them: I am the Lord your God". Lev. 20:6, 27 "And the person who turns to mediums and familiar spirits to prostitute himself with them, I will set My face against that person and cut him off from his people". [27] "A man or a woman who is a medium or who has familiar spirit, shall surely be put to death; they shall stone them with stones. Their blood shall be upon them". All these are abomination to God. Lies, cursing, hatred, backbiting, grudge in heart, homosexuality, fornication, adultery, murder, etc. Lev. 19:11-18. "Also if a man lies with a man as with a woman both of them have committed an abomination, they shall surely be put to death. Their blood shall be upon them". All these are the fruit of idol worship. Idol worship is one of the greatest offense against God the creator of the universe. God created man in His image therefore worshipping of idols means that man had belittled himself and made God a liar and as such God becomes angry for disrespecting and belittling God. God had in many ways warn us to refrain from idol worshipping. God warned the Israelites not to make images of any kind and not to bow down and serve them. After all the miracles and wonders God did, they easily forgot and turned from God to make a CALF and worshipped and sacrifice to, and made God wish to wipe them off the face of the earth. Idol worship is rebellion which is the root of witchcraft and is absolutely stubbornness which is sin. It leads to bloodshed and human sacrifices.

QUESTION: How do we overcome SIN?

We can overcome SIN by the following with their supporting scriptures:

1. By the blood of Jesus Christ: John 5:6, Acts 20:28, Rom. 5:9, Rev. 12:11, Matt. 26:28, 1Pet. 1:18-19, Herb, 9:13-14, 20, 22, 28, Hebr. 10:12.
2. By the Flesh [body] of Jesus Christ: John 6: 27, 33, 48-51, 53
3. By the word of God, **[read, believe and live with the word]**: Hebr. 4:12, 1John 5:7, Eph. 6:16.
4. By the prayer of the righteous, [make solemn or reverent petition to God for help. It can be worship, praises, thanksgiving, confession, repentance, intercession request etc.]: Eph. 6:18, Matt. 26:41, Luk. 22:46, Matt. 6:5, Luk. 18:1, Jonah 2:1, Thess. 5:17, 1Tim. 2:8.

5. By fasting occasionally: Esther 4:16, Ezra 8:23, Daniel 9:3, Jonah 3:5.

6. By obedience to the voice of the Holy Spirit: Exo. 23: 20-22, Exo. 3:2, Acts 8:26, Acts 10:13, Acts 11:11, 12:7. Sin is very powerful and that is the only way to overcome it.

Child Training

BIIBLE QUOTATIOBS: Prov. 29:17, 13:24, 3:11-12, 22:6, 19:18, 6:23, 10:1-3, 23:19-21, 4:10,20, 7:1, Deut. 6:7, 5:16, 8:5, Eph. 6:1-4, Colo. 3:20-21, Exo. 20:12, Lev. 19:3, 1Kings 2:1-4.

Child training has nothing to do with bearing children. You can have children and might not know how to bring them up. Feeding kids and sending them to school every morning is not the only training for children, it does not constitute the best future of children. But teaching them to do things for themselves or himself and helping him to behave and speak with intellect and dignity towards and in public is what is desirable of a trained child. Prov. 6:22. "says train up a child the way he should go and when he is old he will depart from it." So children need direction from parents and one thing we have to know is it takes a community to bring up a child. The parents only is not enough because the parents will not be able to see everything the child does.

The community is the catalytic factor in the life of the child. The parents attitude towards the community is essential. Prov. 3:11-12. "My son despise not the chastening of the Lord neither be weary of this correction. Even as a father, the son in whom he delight". The Lord represents the community, so parents should not be mad, when the community correct the child. Prov. 19:18 says, "Chasten the son while there is hope and let not thy soul spare for his crying". Most parents train their children with leniency and fear which will end up in destroying the child's life or future and will blame the parents when he is old, simple because he lacked certain qualities which the parent did not impart to him, because of leniency, eg." He will stop when he is old or it will take time for him to stop." Meanwhile no effort was made to correct the child from wrong direction. Especially when the community is involve, the parents could even make it a police case as child abuse which could be wrong. Eph. 6:1-3. "Children obey your parents in the Lord for this is right, honor thy father and thy mother which is the first commandment with promise. And ye fathers provoke not your children to wrath but bring them up in the nurture and admonishing of the Lord."

It is the duty of the parents to help the children to grow with certain qualities and never depart from it. The children after the parents had brought them up, it is authentic the children will have to respect the parents as the scripture says. It is the right thing for them to do and as the fifth of the commandments which promise them full capacity to live their full days on earth, if they observe and obey their parents, Deut. 6:7 says, "And thou shall teach them delightly unto the children and shall talk of them when thou sits in thine house and when thou walk in the way and when thou lies down and when thou rise up." The father's protection spiritually and physically becomes a hedge of the child that no one harms him. He also provides for the family table and give direction to the future of the child's life. He corrects the child when he is going the wrong way or path. The mother contribute love towards the child. Therefore when parents themselves do not understand their marriage and are always at loggerhead, it is likely the marriage will not stand and future of the child or the children will be jeopardize.

When parents do not know why they are married and what they are doing, then the marriage will end up in pain and bitterness and will destroy their children's well being or future. This is the more reason why couples must receive marriage counseling before their marriage vows, which is PRE-MARITAL COUNSELING and after the wedding must also receive counseling every five years maximum duration and two years as minimum duration but could decide to receive counseling once every year depending on the couple. This counseling is known as POST-MARRIAGE COUNSELING. The marriage becomes more secured because it raises the couple's academic standard in the marriage and makes them understand the marriage both spiritually and physically, which helps them to be committed and responsible. Post marital counseling help to mend and repair the broken pillars or foundation of the marriage. It is the strength of the marriage and the strength and well being of the children, the main foundation of the life and the future of the children.

CHANGE

Change is an important ornament either in humans or in nations. Without change the statistic improvement of a person or nation will be buried. Roman 12:1-2 "I beseech you therefore brethren by the mercies of God that you present your bodies a living sacrifice, holy, and acceptable to God which is your reasonable service. And do not be conformed to the world but be transformed by the renewing of your minds that you may prove what is that good and acceptable and perfect will of God."

When we present our bodies as living sacrifice, holy and acceptable to God and that is best service we can give to God. When we do not conform to this world governing system, then we are transformed and our minds are renewed. Renewal of our minds is transformation.

Transformation is a change which brings about growth. In otherwise when someone grows, he must develop and that development must bring about prosperity. Prosperity from God has no impediments and sorrow Prov. 10:22. "The blessing of the Lord makes one rich and He add no sorrow with it." It will automatically stay to glorify God. Anything which has no change does not grow and anything that does not grow cannot develop. Someone who is not prepared to change is not prepared to grow and will not develop. Development brings about prosperity and that person or nation which does not want to change and cannot grow to develop is an outcast to prosperity.

One funny thing is people want to prosper without developing, but know that you cannot reach the top of the mountain without climbing, you have to do some climbing to reach the top. Pastor preach about prosperity which is good, without preaching change, growth and development. Yes manna can happen but how often and how many people are blessed enough to receive such manna in this our time. We need to develop to prosper. How can we prosper without growth and developing. Nations remain poor because they do not want to change and because they do not want change, they cannot develop therefore they remain poor and join the EPIC (ending poverty in community) and they have no respect in the world's economic system among nations. So if one want to prosper then he must be prepared for a change.

To have a change one has to encounter with God. It is God who will give the person heart for that change, He is the one who help us in all that we do, on our jobs and every day activities. In Moses era God sent manna but in this time of grace, we are in era of action, God will help us only when we take action. It is the desire of God to give us a future, hope and peace and not affliction, oppression and evil, Jeremiah 29:11. In Isaiah 41:10 says "Fear not, for I am with you. Be not dismay, for I am your God, I will strengthen you Yes I will help you, I will uphold you with My righteous right hand." So this time of grace do not expect manna from heaven but He is your God, your help, your strength and your health. God is ready to help everyone for change to grow unto development and make you prosper and be prosperous and proper. Development brings about invention and creation which leads one to prosperity. Change is development and it leads to growth which is a valuable component that brings quantity from quality. When we have quality we can produce in quantity.

When you walk with God, no matter what you are or who you are, your name will change. Abram walked with God and his name was changed to Abraham. Likewise Sarai walked with God and her name was changed to Sarah and Jacob when he walked with God, his name was changed to Israel. These people encountered with God and their names were changed. Encountering with God cause a change in one's life. Genesis 17:15-16; Genesis 32:26; Genesis35:10-11; Genesis 17: 5-6. As a Christian you have also encountered with Christ so you must also have a change and develop, Eph. 4:23: "And be renewed in the spirit of your mind": This will enable you to have a change of mind, and when you have change of mind, you will:

1. discover your purpose in the world,
2. recover your purpose in the world,
3. fulfill your purpose in the world and,
4. subdue your purpose and have dominion of your purpose in the world.

Moses discovered his purpose and encountered with God, who helped him to change, cause growth in his life, developed and prospered and was able to fulfilled his purpose. He had a royal lifestyle but obtained a godly lifestyle by the hand of God.

Matt. 9:17 says "Nor do they put new wine into old wineskins or else the wineskin breaks, the wine is spilled and the wineskin are wasted. But they put new wine into new wineskins and then both are preserved." It is just saying that when the new wine is put into a bottle, fermentation occur and pressure is built up so change has occurred. If it is an old bottle, it will not be able to withstand the pressure and will explode, but if it is a new bottle it will be able to withstand the pressure and both the bottle and the wine will be preserved. Likewise when we accept Christ and His word be in our new bodies there will be a change in our lives and will result in our growth and development, and prosperity will begins to show up. God is ready waiting for us to avail ourselves to pour fresh oil in us but that fresh oil cannot be poured into the old man, it is our duty to present a new man so God can fill the new body with the fresh oil, which brings about creations and inventions and give us the heart to produce it. Gen. 1:28 says, "Then God blessed them, and God said to them, Be fruitful and multiply; fill the earth and subdue it, have dominion over the fish of the sea, the birds of the air, and over every living thing that moves on earth." God wants every human being to be successful, therefore He wants us to live in His glory, successful in His abundance not poverty in His abundance. He wants us to invent and produce and fill the earth with our invention and be known all over the world, and become spiritually, physically and financially successful, then God will be glorified because He has created us for His glory so that the prophecy of being fruitful and multiply, and fill the earth and subdue to have dominion, shall come to pass. Then God becomes a true and faithful God who honors His word. It is the change, the growth, the development and the prosperity in our lives that proves the existence of God and His faithfulness in our lives. God sees no failure in us but because we do not love God that's why we see failure in our lives. He sees us as His kind. In God there is no failure, so be in God and see no failure of sickness, disappointment, affliction, oppression, infirmity, poverty, mental and physical illness and so on. Man is created the image of God as in Gen. 1:26-27." And God said, Let us make man in our image according to our likeness; let them have dominion over the fish of the sea, over the birds of the air, and over cattle, over all the earth and over every creeping thing that creeps on the earth." So God created man in His own image; in the image of God He created him; male and female He created them." He created us with the dignity to invent and to transcend.

Roman 6:1-18 says "What shall we say then? Shall we continue in sin that grace may abound. And having being set free from sin you may become slaves of righteousness." therefore we sin, if we do not implement the gift God has given to us through the change, as we have been set free from sin, now we become the truth of His blessing, which will give Him all the praise and adoration. No human being is created poor because every being is precious in the sight of God, and is full of talents and riches.

Hence if we seek for change, there will be growth which will bring about development and finally prosperity will be the end result.

CHAPTER FOUR

The Anointing Of God

MEMORY VERSE:- Romans 10:14-154:7-14 and 2-4. Acts 2:2-4. Exodus 30:22-25.

What is this anointing?

It is the result of the physical display of the presence of God upon us, the awareness of His presence. That is the significance of the expression of unseen creator which dwell in unapproachable light, identifying Himself that He had come in the mist of His people, in the manifestation of His love. This manifestation of His love, always proves of His power and the miracles of His might. God gives his anointing for a purpose. The anointing is to set one apart and empower God's elect for the mission He intend to achieve. The setting apart of kings, priests, prophets.etc. the anointing makes this purpose of God extra-ordinary. God passes through the elect to say what He wants to tell his people and also to perform his miracle among His children. Anointing is the physical aspect of the Spirit of God or the Holy Ghost.

THERE ARE TWO KINDS OF ANOINTING:

1. Physical Anointing:- Involve in ministering with oil from the olive, Judges 9:8-9.
2. Spiritual Anointing:- Involve basically with the Holy Ghost, Acts 2:4

PHYSICAL ANOINTING FROM GOD.

The old and the new testament all talk about anointing as well. But the old testament is more of physical anointing with oil specially prepared of the authority and direction of God [to Moses], for the anointing of God's elected people and things of divinity in the house of God. Exodus 30:22-30. God instructed Moses to prepare the holy anointing oil for the anointing of his elect and the alter and things of God and tabernacle.

Leviticus 8:l0-12 Moses through him the anointing oil was made and spirit of God came upon those elect (Aaron and his sons). 1Samuel 10:1 Samuel poured vial of oil on the head of Saul for the Lords anointing as the king to the Lord's children. 1Samuel 10:10-12 The spirit of the Lord came upon Saul after the anointing and he prophesized among the prophets. 1Samuel 16:13 David anointed by Samuel due to instruction of God, with a horn of oil. 1Kings 19:15-17 Hazael, Jehu and Elisha appointed to be anointed by Elijah according to Gods command. 1Kings 1:39 Solomon anointed by Zodak as instructed with a horn of anointing oil. 2Kings 11:12 Joash anointed king. 2Kings 23-30 Jehoahaz anointed as king. From the old testament we see the anointing of priest, prophets, and kings which was a physical anointing with oil made according to instructions God gave to Moses and the prophets. This anointing with oil was sanctification which sets apart and fill the person with the Spirit of God for the Lords service. If the person disobeyed God, then he is no longer under that anointing. 1Samuel 16:14 But the spirit of God departed from Saul.

SPIRITUAL ANOINTING

This is the anointing of the new testament which is given to those called to God by his grace. We no longer live under the law, but under the grace of God. Jesus could not commence his ministry until the anointed came upon Him, the Holy Spirit has to come upon Him and whenever the Holy Spirit comes upon us we see a physical sign. Matt. 3:16-17 Jesus was baptized and the Holy Spirit came upon Him. Luke 4:18-19 (Isaiah 61:1-2) We need the anointing of God to preach the word of God. The spirit of the Lord is upon me.

1. Because He has anointed me to preach the gospel to the poor-meaning all must hear the gospel and no partiality.
2. He has sent me to heal the broken hearted, give hope to the hopeless.
3. To preach deliverance to the captive. the preaching must deliver the captive.
4. And recover of sight to the blind. The blind must receive his sight.

5. To set at liberty those who are oppressed. The oppressed will have his freedom.

6. And to preach the acceptable year of the Lord. The period of grace and peace.

Without the anointing, none of these we can do. Our Lord and Savior Jesus Christ is saying we must be elected by God and be anointed for his purpose, so that we shall be able to perform that duty of which we are elected. Acts 1:4-8. But election comes when we freely open our heart to receive the gift of this grace.

In times pass

1. It was the rich the great men, and the Elders who hear the scripture, but this time of grace all are receiving and hearing the gospel

2. The priest took instruction from God and communicated only with the kings, the rich and the elders to take counsel, John 11:46-54. Caiaphas. but in this time of grace ordinary people are made elders and pastors

3. In the old testament, those with curse died with it, No hope, but in this new testament era we have hope. Luke 13:11-16, the woman with infirmity received healing, Mark 5:2-19 the madman with his dwelling among the tombs regained himself to once again live among the living. The impotent man from birth raised to walk on his feet.. Acts 3:1-9 and 4:9. all these are examples of the hope Jesus Christ has granted us, through the anointing.

4. The blind had no hope, but in this new testament era he has. Mark 10:46-57. Bartimaeus, the blind man received his sight.

5. The poor was always poor, they had no hope for the future. By Jesus Christ those who believed in Him have hope for a better future. 2Cor. 8:9 For ye know the grace of our Lord Jesus Christ that, though he was rich, yet for your sake he became poor, that ye through His poverty might be rich. Christ has already taken care of your poverty, so you are not poor anymore. Jeremiah said in Jer. 29:11 For I know the thought I think toward you, saith the Lord, thoughts of peace, and not evil, to give you an expected end. Bad future could be change to a good future,

a. By the grace of Christ,   b. By the mercy of Christ,   c. By the power of Christ,   d. By the anointing of the Holy Spirit, Acts 4:7-14 and 2-4. Acts 2:29-41.   e. By the blood of Jesus Christ,

We can change dreadful situations and turn the whole thing from anti-clockwise to clockwise. Without the anointing of the Holy Ghost and the power of the blood of Jesus Christ none of these we can do, so Christ is saying we must be elected by God and be anointed for his purpose, so that we shall be able to perform that duty of which we are elected. John 20:22; Acts 4:31. Where there is the anointing of God there is the Holy Spirit, the Holy Spirit is the anointing so when the anointing come upon us the Holy Spirit himself has come upon us. Acts 2:2-4. Therefore a Ministry without the Holy Spirit is like soup without salt, the ministry might not be for Christ. John 16:7, 15:26-27. Luke 4:32. "And they were astonished at his teaching for his word was with authority." When we preach the word of God with authority which come from the Holy Spirit.

1. demons cry   2. demons scatter   3. demons tremble

Luke 4:40-44 1. Jesus did these miracles due to the anointing upon him. 2. The anointing of God which is the presence of the Holy Spirit is an essential requisite manifestation to every ministry of Jesus Christ.

1John 2:20 But ye have an anointing from the Holy one, and ye know all things. - It is the anointing of God that reveals things in the spiritual realm to us. 1John 2:27 "But the anointing which ye have received from him abide in you and you do not need that anyone teaches you; but as the same anointing teaches you concerning all things and is true and is not a lie and just as it has taught you, you shall abide in him."

When we have the presence of the Holy Spirit upon us, we have supernatural knowledge. Without the anointing we shall not be able to learn things of the spirit and through the anointing we know the gifts of the Holy Spirit which are;

1.   The gift of the word of wisdom.
2.   The gift of the word of knowledge

3. The gift of faith.
4. The gift of healing.
5. The gift of the working of miracles.
6. The gift of prophecy.
7. The gift of discernment.
8. The gift of kinds of tongues.
9. The gift of interpretation of tongues.

It is the anointing through which the Holy Spirit opens to us all the scriptures and teaches us from the scripture concerning all things. 1Cor. 14:1-5.

The promise is it for every Christian? Mark 16:16-18. "He that believeth and is baptized shall be saved, but he that believeth not shall be damned. And those signs shall follow them that believe. In my name shall they cast out devils, they shall speak with new tongues, they shall take up serpents, and if they drink any deadly thing, it shall not hurt them, they shall lay hands on the sick and they shall recover." We have to understand that these will not follow the believer, without the spirit which is the baptism of the Holy Spirit. The bible says he that believeth and is baptized, and a Christian must be baptized in Christ and made acceptable to Christ, these signs shall follow him, at least one of these gifts must be seen with him which is anointing of God.

How do we come to know this anointing? First of all, we must understand the scriptural background of the anointing. All the anointing God made upon his elected people, kings, priest, and prophets through his servants was to set apart those elected people for Gods assignment and the manifestation attached. The setting apart is the identification of the anointing.

What about the believer? We live under the new testament or new covenant and we have been called by God's grace for a purpose and without the anointing that purpose cannot be achieved, so the believer also needs the anointing. 2Cor. 1:21. "Now he who establishes us with you in Christ and has anointed us is God." We are clearly told that God has both established us and anointed us (set us apart in Christ for his purpose) (1John 2:20).

How is this establishment and anointing happened? Jesus said that unless one is born again he cannot see the kingdom of God (John 3:3). For a man to enter into the kingdom of God he must be born of water (water baptism) and of the spirit of God [the holy spirit baptism] which is a second birth after our birth by our mothers which is the physical birth. It is the 2nd birth that brings the Holy Spirit upon us who lead us into the kingdom of God and by this we clearly see the establishment and the anointing.

How many times can we receive the anointing? We can receive the anointing as many times possible, meaning charging the anointing. The apostles were filled 3 times:

1. Jesus breathed on them (John20:22).
2. They were filled (Acts 2:4).
3. They were filled again (Acts 4:31).

TRANSFER OFANOINTING THROUGH CLOTHES AND GARMENTS. The believe in the transfer of anointing and healing power through clothing and garments are clearly written in the holy bible. People who do not believe, to them it is stupidity and absolutely craziness and they will have no part in this blessing, of this wonderful supernatural powers. 1. 1Kings 19:19 2. Acts 19:11-12 3. Matt. 14:36 4. Mark 5:27-28, 2Kings 2:13-15.

TRANSFER OF ANOINTING THROUGH LAYING ON OF HANDS. That is the primary application of the impartation of the supernatural powers of anointing by a man of God to another person who has faith in God. Anyone who believes that by the contact of the hands of the man of God, to his body upon a revelation and word of God will bring about the transfer of the anointing of God, will surely receive it, according to the capacity of his faith.

1. 2Tim. 1:6
2. Deut. 34:9
3. Acts. 13:3
4. 2Tim. 1:14
5. Heb. 6:5-7

TRANSFER OF ANOINTING THROUGH ANOINTING OIL.
Jesus himself instructed the disciples to anoint with oil. Anointing oil
has wonderful power in it, if only people will believe this power. Saul was
anointed by Samuel and the spirit of God came upon him. 1Sam. 10:1.
David was anointed by Samuel and the spirit of God came upon him.
1Sam. 16:12-13. The anointing oil is made of olive oil. This oil has great
potential for healing which is necessary to look for. Judges 9:8-9 "The trees
once went forth to anoint a king over them. And they said to the olive
tree, reign over us! But the olive tree said to them, should I cease giving
my oil, with which they honor God and men, and go to sway over trees."
Even olive tree value the gift of God and cherishes it to be more precious
than any other thing, but human beings value the gift of men than the
gift from God.

1. Mark 6:13
2. Jam. 5:14
3. Lev. 21:12

FAITH IN THE MAN OF GOD. God has elected certain people to
represent Him. He use these people to reveal His thoughts, and also speak
through them to the world or His people. One cannot have faith in God
without believing the man of God. These are pastors, prophets, evangelists,
etc. Luke 7:7-10 2Kings 2:13-15 Mark 5:22-23, 28-29 Acts. 9:38-40 Acts
8:15-17 2Kings 4:1-6 2Kings 5:1-13 Luke 4:25-27. Having faith in the man
of God is the sign of believing in God. The man of God represent God in
the Church, therefore believing in the priest or the pastor, the prophet, the
evangelist, the bible teacher, the apostle, the bishop is having faith in God.
How can one have faith in God when he does not believe the priest or the
pastor. These are the people God use to manifest Himself, so if the church
don't believe in them, the church of course don't believe in God either. God

is found in the church and through the priest God is found. 2Chron. 20:20 So they rose early in the morning and went to the wilderness of Tekoa and as they went out. Jehoshaphat stood and said, Hear me O Judah and you inhabitants of Jerusalem, Believe in the Lord your God and you shall be established, Believe in His prophet and you shall prosper.

THE FIVE FOLD MINISTRY:- [1Cor. 12:28, 9-10; Eph. 4:11]

1. The Apostle is church planter.
2. Prophet is a visionary and a revelationist.
3. The Evangelist is a miracle worker.
4. The Pastor is a healer and a shepherd of the church.
5. The Teacher is a bible Scholar.

THE WIND OF THE HOLY SPIRIT. The Holy Spirit can blow as wind over people to receive the anointing of God for His purpose. John 20:22. "And when He had said this, He breathed on them, and said unto them, RECEIVE YE THE HOLY GHOST." Acts 2:2. "And suddenly there came a sound from heaven as of a rushing mighty wind, and it filled all the house where they were sitting."

DEMONS

INTRODUTION:- Satan is the god of the dark world.

Under Satan are:- 1. the devil (gods), 2. witches and wizards, 3. demons

Devil claim glory for Satan, he is the son of Satan. Devil is the one who possesses objects, shrine and rivers and trees to be worshipped, who claim glory for Satan. It is devil which controls the witches and wizards. Because witches and wizards are acquired, they do not live in lifeless entities. Satan possesses citizens with corruption which is the most dangerous weapon to destroy a nation, which has the potential to collapse a nation. Corruption is witchcraft, a powerful evil spirit, that possesses a nation and collapses it, into completely desolation. Any citizen or native who will rise against the witchcraft of corruption will not live for long or take their offer of wealth to live when that person is too strong for them. The greatest network and medium Satan is using to destroy the world is corruption and wants to make sure the whole world is corrupted, that he will own the world, and Christians are at a great war with Satan. Corruption is direct spirit from Satan. Devil the son of Satan will use the witches and wizards to protect their nation and destroy other nation. Witches and wizards distribute demons according to the desire of devil in the form of adverse situation like: demon of sickness, demon of illness, demon of financial difficulty, demon of court issues, demon of marriage issues, demon of child labor, demon of oppression, demon of child abuse, demon of drug addiction, demon of not finding job, demon of stealing, demon of stupidity and foolishness, demon of murder, demon of spiritual marriage, demon of hatred, demon of humiliation and demon of addiction, demon of fornication, demon of adultery, demon of masturbation, demon of action limitation, demon of jealousy, demon of selfishness, demon of harlotry (Hosea 4:12) and so on, to torment mankind and all come with disgrace and death. The duty of demons is to make life difficult for mankind, afflict and oppress people which takes many forms and years. All these Satan is the master mind of it, because he is jealous of man for the simple reason that man has the opportunity and favor of God. Because God has given his estate on earth to human being through Jesus Christ. That is the reason why Satan is doing everything possible to destroy man. He is using so many networks and mediums to capture human race, purposely to destroy them. **Satan still does not admits his fault and counts on pride, he feels he is better than man because he has only one category with man, we are all created by God but he is spirit as God and does not admit that anyone can judge him. His time is yet to come.** Many at times, people who are possessed by demons, cannot believe until it manifests, some might know but all can be delivered. The spirit of witches and wizards do not possess but they are acquired because those humans like to have them on purpose and agenda. The world is at war with the satanic world. **Demons are unclean spirits and witches and wizards are evil spirit.** One, being the higher that is the spirit of witches and wizards are acquired and the other, being the lesser that is demon is released to possess. The gods are those which cause human beings to worship them, an abomination and the greatest sin in the universe which make God separates. **The gods are direct spirit of Satan.** They are cool and collective, they are not aggressive like the witches and wizards. They also claim glory and when they have to cause havoc, it's a big havoc and disaster. Their havoc could take a whole nation and whole nation could come under its power. These are spirits which possess Rivers, Lakes, Idols, Grooves, Statues, Rocks, Mountains, etc. Because they desire human beings to worship them and they drive human beings into materialism and paganism. They normally do not torment because they receive glory from mankind, but when they desire to cause harm it's big havoc. Witches and wizards, are the smaller and what they do against humanity is they torment people with demons. Demons are the smallest among the spirits. The harm and the havoc demons cause is the smallest. But what we call the smallest, one can imagine the effect. These cause what we call illness, sickness, confusion, addiction, pride, lies, bloodshed, fornication, adultery, emulation, lasciviousness, madness, cancer, ulcer, high blood pressure, kidney failure, stroke, cardiac rest (heart attack), diabetes and the like. The devils known as gods take captive of the witches and wizards to use them. These little evil spirits create panic in mankind. When demons tarry for far too long they will develop and become witches and wizards, which are aggressive and torment the one they have possessed and other innocent human beings. Know that witches and wizards perform evil activities in the life of mankind in the form of situations known as demons. So demon is an evil situation and is a spirit. **WHAT IS A DEMON?** Demon is an unclean spirits. These demons are spirit beings without material or physical body which seek a physical or material body to live in. They do not care whether they live in a person or in an animal, all that they need is to have material body, through which they can express themselves or operate or function or manifest. They can enter into objects when an opportunity is created for them, provided the object or body can serve their purpose. There are so many doors without security in life and when they are liberal, demons become real, Mark 5:7-13. They enter and they will torment that person. We have been made to understand by the power, knowledge and wisdom of Jesus Christ, that these demons could be cast out. Matt.12:43-45, meaning if we as Christians live to the will of God, then these demons will be nothing before Christians. When we command them under proper authority, they must get loosed, come out and depart. The bible says these signs shall follow those who believe and are baptized, in my name they will cast out demons. Mark 16:17. So as Christians we are empowered to do so because we believe in Jesus Christ and we should not be afraid of demons, neither Satan because he, Satan was created by God and we are also created by God so Satan is not better than man. The bible says he that is in us is greater than he that is in the world, that's outside us, 1John 4:4. We have Jesus Christ which Satan does not have. Demons can only be cast out by the name of Jesus Christ, (Luke 9:49-50). Without the name of Jesus no demons could be cast out and they will attack. And to be able to cast out demons, you must be a Christian, believe in Jesus Christ and be baptized and live according to the will of Christ. Acts 19:11-17. **CHARACTER OF DEMONS.** What we have to know is that the will of demon or demons is to possess a physical body through which they can express their purpose and use the material body to operate the way they want. These demons have knowledge that's why when their attempt fail they take another initiative, they think and they reason. In Mark 1:24. those demons knew that Jesus Christ was the Messiah (the holy one of God). Demons are violence, when they were cast out they went into the lake violently and were choked and because they think and reason they can plead so the demons in the madman met Jesus and began pleading with Him to permit them to enter into the swines, if he drove them out of the man. Luke 8:27-30. One thing we as Christians must know is that demons have will, that's the desire to do something. In Matt 12:44-45. the demon took decision to go back and when he was back swept the place and garnished and went and took with him other company of seven who are more wicked than himself – that's reinforcement, a strong defense against any intruder or any army and make sure no one can take possession of the place this time. Demons can speak because in the presence of the Holy Ghost they are compelled to speak, tell their story whatever they have done and whatever intention they have also planned. In Matt. 8:28-29 the bible said, "in the country of Gergesene, there met Jesus two possessed with demons, came out of the tombs with exceeding fierce so that no man might pass by that way and behold they cried out saying (they spoke) what have we to do with thee Jesus, thou son of God? Art thou come thither to torment us before time." They knew they cannot be in that man forever because their time was limited in that man, so you see these demons will one day come out and continue somewhere else but Jesus did not allow them to go and continue somewhere else but eradicate them. Demons do not die but when they have destroyed that body, they evacuate and seek another physical object and possess it, so that they can continue to function. Only Jesus and the name and the blood of Jesus Christ can kill them. They are very cunning, they have believe and they believe that there is God, someone greater than all powers in the universe, who created all things James 2:19, so they can capitalize on this since they knew mankind know and believe that there is God. Upon this they invent stories, create panic and cause people to abandon their faith to follow ungodly teachings and hardening their hearts and indulging in all kinds of impurity. 1Tim. 4:1-2, Eph. 4:19. Whenever we do deliverance we have to kill them by telling them to die in the name of Jesus. Asking them to come out is not enough, is easy for them to possess someone right there. Jesus Christ did not ask the demon to come out and left it, but He said "and have your peace" meaning you can not possess anyone no more. They also speak as the Holy Ghost does and make people obscene from meat, stay away from marriage but practice fornication and homosexuality. Demons also enslave people with fear and harassment. In Acts 17:5-9 the demons possessed the people, that's the infidels to rise against those who heard the word and believed and put Jason in custody, enslaving him.

Temptations is not of God, it is of the devil. Because the bible says, if anyone is tempted, he is not tempted of God. James 1:13. Demons are tricky, they can cause people to lie and sin and bring death unto people, as it happened to Ananiase, Acts 5:1-11, that is enticement, 1Kings 13. They play their wiles on people, and they do not stop tempting because when they rest, Satan will punish them. Matt.26:41 "so we have to watch and pray that we may not enter into temptation. The spirit is willing but the flesh is weak." **Demons are very deceptive.** They deceive some Christians, believers who are baptized and who the Lord's gift has come upon them and give them prideful feeling and deceiving emotion. If we allow ourselves for such emotion to rule our spiritual life, taking the place of the spirit of God in us, that emotion will have impact. Those who worship God worship in spirit. If we allow the spirit of God to rule over our lives, based on the word of God then we will always be able to identify between the spirit of God and demonic spirit. Some believers over react thinking that by so doing, people may believe that they have the spirit of God and put their trust in them. Such believers may feel that they have drawn attention by shaking and jerking of their body and the shivering of their palms and arms and their unprecedented prophecies which sometimes become bored and cause confusion because they give long prophecies which most at times are planned prophecies, which cause trouble in the church. They may also think that they are trying to impress people, especially visitor or new comers, to proof that they have special anointing from the Holy Ghost. These are not from the spirit of God but demonic from the flesh, combining the gift of God with the gift of Satan- the deceiving spirit or spirit of deception. **The spirit of shock** is one of the dangerous spirits, it can kill instantly no matter who you are, once it possesses you, reduces your emotions, brings coldness in you, give you fear and begins to dominate your brain, transmitting the fear to your heart and finally stops the heart. Shock is a demon. Demons do torment humans. Churches claim superiority over other churches, this is demonic influence. If we believe that all churches belong to Jesus Christ then no one has any right to claim superiority. Demons are working seriously and hard for Satan and if Christians should work at that rate, one can imagine what a peace we can bring to the world. Demons can possess any of these persons, a pastors, apostles, evangelist, teachers, prophets, bishops, etc. in short the modern day men of God to do evil. A pastor or an apostle will not like his brother apostle to be equal or do better than him, he will always find a means to cripple the other apostle or the pastor, especially when that apostle is senior and the other apostle is his associate. All these are demonic influences and power. So if such pastor or evangelist or apostle cast out demons, what is he trying to portray or displaying to the church. Oppression, suppression, humiliation, torment are equally the same spirit, they are all demons, Luke 13:14-15, 31-33. Sometimes a pastor will be so sincere to accept another pastor into his ministry and after some time the other pastor will break the church into two and take half of the members away to plant his own church, that's DEMON OF SEPARATION, very powerful, violence and dangerous and easily murder. We can see this by the notion behind the separation, its for money. **TERROR OF DEMONS.** Demons join with witches and wizards to make war among nations by their supernatural strength. War in our time, physical war and spiritual war, is not of God, therefore no one should relate war to be the revelation of God. Who can withstand His anger. He will fight the opponent with natural disasters, the hurricane will slap that nation, Earthquake will swallow the buildings, volcano will melt the earth and there will be no place for mankind. If it's of God, Jesus would have set an example. It is one of Satan's destructive weapon. In Luke 9:54-56 when the apostles wanted to make war, Jesus said, war was not part of my mission, meaning the apostles did not know the kind of fire they were talking about. Basically struggle for power is of the Satan, the devil and his witches and wizards and demons fight over power, they fight over position, fight over property and they fight over riches, because they have lost their glory, they have no glory with God and now that is their nature, the only way for Satan to acquire glory. When Jesus came he did not fight over these worldly things because they belong to him. Likewise, you as a child of God, being heir of the creator, owns all these things so a Christian need not to fight over worldly things. When demons possess one emotionally, they make sure that person is completely still, feels rejected, lonely as if he has no help, feels he has failed in life, feels like he cannot do it, who am I, my education is too low for the position. By so doing, affecting the attitude of the person and everything this person does will be wrong and eventually he will not attempt to do anything. He will be doubting whatever he will do, he becomes indecision and procrastination and insecure. Demons can affect the tongue to blasphemy, curse people and speak big lies and gossip about everybody they see and everything they hear. Where one of these spirits is found all these five will be found because they walk together (rejection, fear, blasphemy, lies and gossip). They have no fear, you can be a man of God, they can function in you, if you create an opportunity for them. They need tongue to lie. Demons cause people to become smokers, alcoholics, workaholics, anoxia (children born under alcoholic influence with low amount of oxygen). **CONCLUSION.** This is how demons function and operate in and on human beings and now you know how to deal with them. Our environment is full of demons so we should cleave unto the mighty power, **Jesus Christ,** who will give us his spirit to combat with these demons. Because of our unbelief, but if we have faith like the grain of mustard seed we shall say unto this mountain, remove hence to yonder place and it shall remove and nothing shall be impossible unto us. Matt. 17:20.

LAYING ON OF THE HAND

The door of the human body, that's the temple of God is between the forehead and the center of the head, Before you can drive out or cast out a demon possessing a body. This is in most stubborn cases. The key to the door of the body, that is the five fingers, **the finger of grace and the finger of gift on the side veins or the two side shells of the forehead and the finger of truth placed at the middle of the forehead and the finger of power and the finger of victory at the side below the finger of gift.** Now the key of the door of the body is fixed into the door key hole and the moment the demon or whatever it is, is commanded in JESUS name to leave or you tell the demon, to come out of him or her, it comes out. You can bind the demon before asking him to go out of the person, and it comes out immediately, it does not waist time, all in the name of Jesus Christ. Now the two side shells of the forehead is for memorizing and once the finger of grace and the finger of truth and gift are placed on them, you should memorize. The whole palm is for blessing, so if you place the whole palm on top of the forehead that is the fingers of grace, truth, gift, power and victory the blessings begin to enter into the person by the blessing instrument and it is received. 2Timothy 1:6-7 Therefore I remind you to stir up the gift of god which is in you through **the laying on of my hand.** Again, Heb. 6:2 Of the **doctrine** of baptism, **and of laying on of the hands**, and of resurrection of the dead, and of eternal judgment.

1st finger (tomb) is the finger of grace; 2nd finger is the finger of truth; 3rd finger is the finger of gift

4th finger is the finger of power; 5th finger is the finger of victory.

THE FINGER OF GRACE:- This finger bears the compassion of salvation, which is eternal, being the right for every human being to receive. Salvation which is beyond the understanding of man, was highly protected by God and made sure no one will lay hands on it. The grace is the last hope of man. Salvation brings all people neither Greek or Jew, neither black nor white under the same umbrella of Jesus Christ and made us "many people with one mind." Gal. 3:28-29. There is neither Jew nor Greek, there is neither bond nor free, there is neither male nor female, for ye are all One in Christ. And if ye be Christ's, then are ye Abraham's seed, and heirs according to the promise. Eph. 2:8-10 For by grace ye are saved through faith and that not of yourself, it is a gift of God. Not of works lest any man should boast. For we are his workmanship created in Christ Jesus unto good works, which God had ordained that we should walk in them. So that is the work and compassion of grace, the spirit of sanctification. So everyone who has this hope of grace in him is purified and made pure. So sanctification is imparted unto the one upon whom the pastor lays hand.

THE FINGER OF TRUTH:- This finger bears the truth in the word of God, the truth in Christ because only in Christ is truth found and whatever God says is of truth and is not a lie. 1John 2:27 But the anointing which ye have received of him abideth in you, and ye need not any man teach you: but as the same anointing teaches you of all things and is truth and is not a lie and even as it hath taught you, ye shall abide in him.. So this truth brings the love of God, which come with compassion, which kindles us for the works of charity and be help to one another without begrudging none. By such attitude as Christians, we hereby know that we are of the truth and believe that we all shall be before Christ. 2Cor. 5:10. John 14:6 Jesus said unto him, I am the way, the truth and the life, no one cometh unto the father but by me. So truth is found in Jesus Christ and by Jesus we receive the truth. So the finger of truth impart the truth in Christ unto the one whom the pastor has laid the finger of truth on. This truth enables us to know Christ. John 14:7. If you had known Me, you would have known My Father also; and from now on You know Him and have seen Him.

THE FINGER OF GIFT:- *1Cor. 12:1-11* 1. Now concerning spiritual, brethren, I would not have you ignorant. Ye know that ye were Gentiles carried away unto those dump idols even as ye were led. Wherefore I give you to understand that no man speaking with the spirit of God called Jesus accurse, and that no man can say that Jesus is the Lord but by the Holy Ghost. Now there are diversities of gifts, but the same spirit. And there are differences of administration but the same Lord. And there are diversities of operations but it is the same God which worketh all in all. But the manifestation of the spirit is given to every man to profit withal. For to one is give by the spirit. 1. THE WORD OF WISDOM; 2. THE WORD OF KNOWLEDGE; 3. FAITH; 4. HEALING; 5. MIRACLES; 6. PROPHECY; 7. DISCERNING OF SPIRITS 8. DIVERSE KINDS OF TONGUES 9. INTERPRETATION OF TONGUES. But all these works that one and selfsame spirit, dividing to every man severally as he will. So that is what we experience when the finger of gift is laid on a believer.

FINGER OF POWER:- 1Cor. 1:24 But unto them which are called both Jews and Greeks, Christ the power of God, and The wisdom of God. So we see that Christ is the power, therefore the finger of power impart the anointing of Christ and the Holy Ghost to the person, which has the ability to take out these spirits, sickness, divorce, poverty, homelessness, joblessness etc. and the person gets his breakthrough. We all know power is the manifestation of the ability to do something. So there will be no power manifestation if there is no action. As soon as the power of God come upon us we become active in whatever work we are called to do.

THE FINGER OF VICTORY:- Rom. 8:37 Nay, in all these things we are more than conquerors [victors] Through him [Jesus] that loves us. Our God, the Living God loved us unto death and the bible says, nothing can separate us from the love of Christ, neither death nor life, nor angels, nor principalities, nor powers, nor present things, nor things to come. Because Our victory is in Christ Jesus and the scripture says if God be for us who can come against us. We are in Christ who is the master conqueror and by His name and blood, we have victory. We can do all things by Christ which strengthen us. So with this finger victory is achieved.

THE REAL ASPECT OF CHRIST

The bible says for him all things were made and by him all things were made. And God said to Christ (the Prince) the ruler of the kingdom of Heaven, as the bible testifies in Jn. 1:1 and Jn. 1:14: In the beginning was the word and the word was with God and the word was God. And the word was made flesh and dwelt among us, and we beheld his glory, the glory as of the only begotten son of the father full of grace and truth. So said God the Father to Christ, Satan has corrupted the earth and now rules the planet that I love, the planet of my heart. Satan has led the whole earth into suffering, problems, sickness, killing, molestation, bulling and more, which is the result of corruption. Satan has filled the earth with evil. Man is now a slave to devil. God then said to Christ, then I am delegating you (Christ) to go (Eze. 22:30) and teach the whole earth how they could overcome Satan and save the whole earth with your blood, because your blood will be a terror on Satan, In. (Mk. 2:28 and Mt. 9:38). Christ the Lord of the harvest and the Lord of the Sabbath, accepted the challenge. What happened, in the kingdom of heaven? As soon as Christ accepted the challenge from the father to come to the earth to save man from his sins, to save man from the bondage of Satan, the whole atmosphere of the kingdom of heaven turned to the color of gold. Michael and his battalion matched through the streets and the whole population of angels jubilated singing and dancing in the kingdom saying, "Glory be to God in the highest. Why? Because the son of God has accepted to sacrifice to the father's will to rescue the captive, the lost and the kingdom on earth. God then said to Christ, you now bear my name as a son, I God your father in you and you CHRIST in me. You have my holy spirit, and my holy spirit is in You and always with you for ever. Jn. 14:10-11. God then said to Christ, after you have come back your decision in this kingdom is final and nothing else. Only you and you alone, even I your father has nothing to say, for this Jesus said in: JOHN. 14: 13 - 16; Whatsoever ye shall ask in my name, that I will do, that the father may be glorified in the son. If ye shall ask anything in my name, I will do it. If ye love me keep my commandments. And I will pray the father and he will give you another comforter that he may abide with you forever. Jesus also said in JOHN. 10: 17-18; Therefore doth my father love me, because I lay down my life, that I might take it again. No man takes it from me, but I lay it down of myself. I have power to lay it down and I have power to take it again This commandment have I received from my father. AMEN.

God said to Christ no single person will be left on earth if I should appear on the earth. Christ then said to God His father, if I Christ, I am to appear on earth in spirit, the people I am going to save cannot bear my appearance, because things that will happen to purify the earth, before my appearance will be too hectic beginning with storm, earthquake, volcanoes, thunderstorms and lightening etc. to clean up the earth of every sin for six days, and the seventh day my appearance, Rev.16:18, so I Christ will like to appear on the earth in the human form, conceived nine months and through the human process. God the father also accepted. John 3: 16 - 17. "For God so love the world that he gave his only begotten son, that whosoever believeth in him should not perish, but have everlasting life. For God sent not his son into the world to condemned the world, but that the world through him might be saved." Jesus is really the SON of God, if you believe it or not. He is God because the son of a king is also a king (he is the next king) so the Son of God is also God. So this way Christ came to the earth. Luke 1: 26-30 says: "And in the sixth month the angel Gabriel, was sent from God unto a city of Galilee named Nazareth. To a virgin espoused to a man whose name was Joseph of the house of David. And the virgin's name was Mary. And the angel came in unto her and said, HAIL, thou that art highly favored, the Lord is with thee, Blessed art thou among women. And when she saw him she was troubled at his saying, and then taught in her mind what manner of salutation this should be and the angel said unto her, fear not Mary, for thou has found favor with God. Thou shall conceive and bring forth a son and shall be called JESUS." As soon as JESUS CHRIST was born unto the earth, the seven curtains dividing the earth and Heaven was broken to allow communication between Christ and God alone. All other communication between God and all prophets was closed. And Heaven and Earth became visible to each other. The whole angels of the kingdom of Heaven were seen singing songs of praises, saying "glory be to God in the highest," because "THE LORD" the son of God was born unto the earth. The bible confirms this: Luke 2: 11-14." For unto you is born this day in the city of David a savior, which is Christ the Lord. And this shall be a sign unto you, ye shall find the baby wrapped in swaddling clothes lying in a manger. And suddenly there was a multitude of the heavenly host praising God and saying Glory to God in the highest and on earth peace and good will towards men."

That day Satan and his demons, all over the universe song songs of praises because God has come down with power and authority, thinking the mistake of Adam still exists. But watch, the evil spirit and Satan their boss were deprived, no power or authority allotted them and the name of Jesus Christ became a terror upon Satan and his host, that is why Jesus Christ said when you bind the devil, bind him in my name. Jesus did not come for war with man so the angelic host with him always obeyed his instruction and never for the sake of Christ, angels attacked man till he returned to his seat. For this Jesus Christ advice us not to fight against blood neither against flesh but to love one another. Ephesians 6: 12. "For we wrestle not against flesh and blood but against principalities, against powers, against the ruler of darkness of this world, spiritual wickedness in the high places." Jesus Christ is the God whom the father has given all the authority and power both in Heaven and on the Earth. Matth. 28:18 and Matth. 11:27. Without him we shall not see the father and when we see Jesus Christ, we see the father. Salvation was the mission of God and for this Christ came to the earth. Jesus gave himself to be arrested and be crucified as the bible states: that which is written in the scripture might be fulfilled. John 18:4-9. and Isaiah 53:7,10.

As soon as Jesus Christ was arrested, the angels in Heaven began to sing songs of praises saying, "OUR GOD IS ABOUT TO CONQUER THE WORLD." He is the greatest warrior, till the time he was crucified. There was heavy rainfall which was not for fancy, it has significance which stands for purification. Immediately Jesus Christ breathed his last breath as he cried out and gave up his soul, the atmosphere of Heaven became diamond pure white and angels descending to welcome Jesus Christ saying,

THIS IS OUR GOD THE KING OF THE UNIVERSE, PRAISE THE LORD AND PRAISE HIS NAME. CHRIST JESUS IS THE GOD

WHOM THE FATHER HAS GIVEN THE AUTHORITY AND POWER BOTH ON EARTH AND IN HEAVEN.WITHOUT HIM WE SHALL NOT SEE THE FATHER, WHEN WE SEE HIM, WE SEE THE FATHER. AMEN.

This went on until Jesus rose from the death. The angels waited in songs of praises until Jesus had completely finished his job on earth, both in the grave and on the surface of the earth. The father honored him with great honor. He was accompanied in mezzo of the angels with songs of praises to his throne. When a spear was pierced in the side of Jesus, he oozed blood unto the earth. The blood that dropped unto the earth spread and covered the whole earth. In this wise Jesus bought the sins of the whole world with his own blood, and died for every human being and for the world's salvation, and the third day, rose to life. Jesus Christ promised and did it. Matt.17:9, 22-23. "And as they came down from the mountain, Jesus charged them saying: Tell the vision to no man, until the son of man be risen again from the dead. And while they abode in Galilee, Jesus said unto them, the son of man shall be betrayed into the hands of men, and they shall kill him and the third day he shall be raised again, and they were exceedingly sorry." Amen.

After his resurrection he then went to meet his disciples on many occasion and performed miracles. After that wherever there were Jews (Israelites), Jesus appeared unto them and appointed his disciples among them whom he gave authority to continue with the work of God to baptize, to teach and to protect the Israelites. As we have learnt, the blood of Jesus is a terror on Satan and his son the devil. When we bind him, with the blood of Jesus, Satan becomes congested and begins to struggle, when we continue to bind him, he is conquered. Jesus set foot on the land, the river, the sea, these has purpose. Why? Because his blood had to save the world as the father had commanded, therefore if one should live on the sea, since Jesus had set foot on the sea, his blood will spread to wherever he had set foot to save all. Jesus loves all and he is the savior of all. No one has ever seen God, even the angels, with exception of Christ Jesus. Jesus Christ the love of God is the only one, who do sits with God the father, and knows the father. John 6: 46. The angels do hear the voice of God, but do not see his face. John

1:18." No one has seen God at any time. The only begotten Son, who is in the bosom of the Father, He has declared Him." Angels take instruction from God, converse with him but no one of them can tell how God is. Therefore whatever you need, is better you ask from Jesus Christ and better still ask from God in the name of Jesus Christ. Request directly to God do not come as we wish. Request to God through Jesus Christ yields immediate result or a little while after. Let's put our faith in Jesus Christ and we shall see the power of God. The help we are looking for is close to our feet but because is on our feet we do not regard it. So to-day you know where you should direct your prayer and whom your prayer goes, and to what office your demand is directed and when to expect an answer. I hope you have taken Jesus Christ as you savior so you will have what you want in the name of Jesus. This is the Christ, God the son, the living God who is the most popular since the creation of the universe. He did not write a single book but has more books than ever and over all mankind, he did not write songs but has more songs in his name than all in the universe. This is the real aspect of the man, Christ Jesus.

BEWARE, SATAN IS STILL AT WORK

God's desire was to have a human family in his likeness and image, to share his life and love that he could make fellowship with his physical family who will continue with the rest of his creation, that HE, God would appear physically and move in his glory in the responsibilities of man. But man denied himself and came under bondage. After God had created the earth and all was set, there was the need of someone to care for the earth, so the bible says in:-

Gen. 2:5 And there was not a man to till the ground. This means there was not an someone to work on the surface of the earth. God would have put an angel to take care of the earth. God decided to put a physical being at the care of his physical creation because:-

1. God needed a physical being and not a spirit being to take care of the physical creation.
2. Due to the behavior of Lucifer the chief angel who is now called Satan, God loved man more than the angels and gave power to man, power which is more potent than that of the angel.

The bible confirms this because there had not been any occasion in the bible where God blessed the angels and gave dominion to them to subdue the earth but God gave power to man.

The bible confirms this in:- Gen.1:28 And God blessed them and said unto them: 1. Be fruitful 2. And multiply 3. Replenish the earth 4. Subdue the earth 5. And have dominion over the fish of the sea, and over the fowl of the air, and over every living thing that moves upon the earth.

This shows that there is abundant power, an unlimited power stored in man by the almighty God, because of the great responsibility which is put before man by the creator of the universe. God is power and power belongs to God alone. God gives power to whom he had ordained to assume his responsibilities meant for. When God created us, He knew us before creation. Jeremiah 1:5. "Before I formed thee in the belly I knew thee, and before thou comest forth out of the womb I sanctify thee, and I ordained thee a prophet unto the nation." So God knew the responsibilities He had for man. God then commune with his board of directors, that's the prince of the Universe, both Heaven and Earth, Christ Jesus and his adviser, the Holy Ghost, the Fire Works. So it is writing in Gen.1:26-27. "And God said let us make man in our image, after our likeness and let them have dominion over the earth and all in it. So God created man in his own image, in the image of God created he him, male and female."

Man is created to take the form of the Lord God the Father, to take the form of Jesus Christ, God the Son, to take the form of God the Holy Ghost. Before man was created, God looked at all the kingdoms of the earth and selected a suitable kingdom for each individual, which is so rich and so loving. But people out of their own mistakes accuse God for nothing, eg. Why God has made me poor? Why am I black? Why me in Africa? Why God made me male or female, I have male or female qualities, I am man not a woman or a woman not a man and that has brought about lesbians and gays which is completely out of the track of human and the purpose of God. People refuse to believe in God and worship Him because of these complains. God is the creator, all things both physical and spiritual were created by him, and that makes Him God. Our faith in God changes nothing about God. God is the same yesterday, today and forever. Hebr. 13:8.

Romans 9:20-21." Nay but, O man, who art thou that replies against God? Shall the things formed say to him that formed it, Why hast thou made me thus? Has not the potter power over the clay, of the same lump to make "one vessel unto honor, and another unto dishonor? What if God, willing to show His wrath, and to make his power known, endured with much longsuffering the vessels of wrath fitted to destruction. And that he might make known the riches of his glory on the vessel of mercy which He had prepared unto glory". Complains will rather worsen the situation because it paves way for the devil to take advantage of your situation. We must be strong and courageous to observe to do the will of God according to the word of God and pray that we shall be made to manifest the God's purpose of creation. And do away completely with unnecessary complains and accusations against God. Only by meditating and implementing God's word in our lives, that we shall make our way prosperous and shall have good success. Complains are enemy to your success and even to your health because it brings jealousy, envy, hatred, wickedness, murdering, etc. These are demons, when allowed to operate in ones life will lead to destruction. Our appearance on earth is so important to God that God does not take off his eyes from us. There is a purpose for every human being on earth to accomplish. God did not send us to this world for fancy sake, Jesus said to his mother, when she said, why have you made us look for you all over the district? Jesus said, "Look for me! don't you know that I have my father's business to perform." We have been sent to the world by our Father to execute and accomplish a particular mission and when we fail to accomplish that mission, we shall be guilty of our act in the world. For example, someone is sent by his government to America to study and come back to account for, and take up a responsibility. But when he came to America, he abandoned his purpose, and took up a job and entered in the dollar harvest, so what he has to become, he could not, when he returns to his country, definitely he will be thrown into prison and his life will be miserable. As a human being in the world you should ask yourself, from where did I come to the world, to where will I return and what is my purpose on earth. The bible says God sent us to the world to do his will but we have taken to our own way which had made God to separate from us but God the son came down to bridge our relationship with the Father that through Jesus Christ we shall surely see the father. So God searched through the world families and placed you in a suitable family, through whom you will be led to the world to assume the responsibilities of God for his glory. God did not create us for fancy sake, but for a purpose. Human beings think we are brought to the world by the knowledge of man, or by the strength of man or by the wisdom of man.

Our first appearance in the womb we never looked like a human being neither a substance but God who is able to do all continued to turned us in the womb till we came to resemble a human being. Our God who is able to do all, continued to be turning this child in the womb till it was time for the child to be delivered to the world. That's not the end. The Lord

God continued to protect the child keeping him growing. No doctor or human being can tell how man continue to grow but God who is always able does it and we became men. God is an intelligent God, all knowing and all seeing. Before He created man, He saw that, the earth was dried and man could not carry on the responsibilities, so He waited and made the earth fruitful by causing rain to moisturize the earth, then man was assigned to continue with the rest of the physical creations, not to the glory of man but to the glory of God. So the bible says God cause rain to fall on the surface of the earth to make his plans complete as read from: Gen. 2:6 "But there went up a mist from the earth and watered the whole face of the ground". So God after searching through all the kingdoms of the earth and putting you in a particular kingdom entrusted power and his responsibilities to man. Every human being in this world was sent by God for a purpose and a mission, and each has his training to receive to acquire a specific profession for the plan of God. You are the one God sent to the world to study medicine so that through you God will provide medicine for AIDS [acquired immune deficiency syndrome] a destructive weapon of Satan, which in human sense, caused by the infection with HIV [human immune-deficiency Virus], to stop its destruction of human race but because you took to your own way, you were not able to achieve that profession and the disease AIDS killed and destroyed millions of human beings. The blood of those who have been taken by AIDS and killed will be required of this person who did not achieved his plan of God. That's the judgment. You are the one God sent to the world to be a great engineer to invent a device to prevent accident on the road but you had abandoned that mission. All lives of those wrongfully killed in accidents which could have been prevented by your device which you are the inventor will be required of you. As a pastor, you have one million souls to save but could not achieve that mission, the blood of those lives will be required of you. God needs to save only one big soul with you so that He, God, can use that soul to save millions of souls but you refused to be a pastor, the blood of those millions to be saved will be required of you. Search through the bible and know your responsibility. You are medical doctor to save life to the glory of God, find out. You are an architect to design complex and beautiful buildings, search for. You are a mechanical engineer to make sophisticated machines to the glory of God, find out. God is going to judge us for abandoning our responsibilities. You are a priest to correct the minds of the people to the glorify God, find out. Because when God gets angry even the righteous will be in trouble. The story of Jonah.

What happens after God has placed us in the womb of our mothers? Any of us know that Satan snatched the dominion and subdued the first man and destroyed him before God. He pushed man into problems, hardship, confusion, financial crisis and things which were not in the destiny of man. Satan not being satisfied is always aggressive and continues to attack who ever God brings to the world to carry out his responsibilities for the glory of God. You know that Satan is always against God and finds means to destroy all good things from God because of his PRIDE. Satan will say I will not let you work for God, come and work for me because I am the ruler of the world, and that's true Satan is ruling the earth. The god of the world. 2Cor. 4:4 "In whom the god of this world hath blinded the minds of them which believed not, lest the light of the glorious gospel of Christ, who is the image of the invisible God, should shine unto them". John. 12:31. "Now is the judgment of the world. Now shall the prince of the world be cast out". And John. 14: 30 "Here after I will not talk much with you for the prince of this world cometh and hath nothing in me". Jesus himself confirmed it that Satan rules the world. Satan after Jesus had chased him out of the earth hides under the sea and sends agents to carry on his duties to destroy lives. Isaiah 27: 1, Psalm 74:13-14. So immediately God finds a suitable family and place man in the womb of the woman, Satan will also send his agents to approach the family and talk to them to misdirect the child's glory God has given to him. This is the message normally from Satan by his agents; 'You are pregnant, you should seek for protection, you know this child must be a great man.' Satan believes that God has created everybody to be great and special, the bible confirms it and Satan will refer as he did to Jesus from Psalm 91 in Luke 4: 10-11 and was defeated, seeking for protection means accepting his offer. The wiles Satan used on Adam and Eve, still holds against this modern generation. We forget that the child was put into the womb by God and the weapon to protect the child is the word of God and our righteousness and prayer. After this couple has surrender to Satan, he begins to laugh at them and becomes happy because this family has surrendered to certain circumstances. And if this family should seek for that protection, if they do, the glory of this child, the power of this child and the dominion God has given to this child for the glory of God is stolen from this child. The child becomes defenseless spiritually, his godly understanding is taken from him. **Satan has a well organized deceptive world administration which he uses to blindfold and take people captive.** He always imitates what God does and produce its counterfeit. Let us listen to the voice of God and let His word influence us as Mary and Joseph did. Luke. 1:30-31 "And the angel said unto her, Fear not, Mary: for thou hast found favor with God. And behold, thou shall conceive in thy womb, and bring forth a son, and shall call his name Jesus". Matt. 1:20-21 "But while he (Joseph) thought on these things, behold, the angel of the Lord appeared unto him in a dream, saying, Joseph, thou son of David, fear not to take unto thee Mary thy wife; for that which is conceived in her is of the Holy Ghost". God sent an angel to appear unto Mary and also in a dream unto Joseph. Satan also do send his agents to carry out his deceit, to give dreams to families, so we have to be careful. Job. 9: 24." The earth is given unto the hand of the wicked: he covers the faces of the judges (the rightful owners) thereof; if not, where, and who is he?' The mistakes Adam and Eve did is still being repeated by us.

Christianity is not for excitement, neither for fancy. Christianity is to learn to function the earth as desired by God, with the requisite knowledge delivered unto Satan by Adam, which Christ has redeemed it back to us. Let us live on the word of God, live on righteousness, pray ceaselessly, draw near to God so that God will also draw near to you, and we shall know why we are in the world, and our children will be great men and women. God is an intelligent God, who created the earth out of nothing, then out of the earth He created Man, and out of the man He created Woman. And out of the man and the woman He had created, comes the present human beings and the present civilization, the developments and sophisticated technologies. Therefore God had also created us to this world to behave as his likeness.

1. to create jobs out of nothing.
2. to create better living conditions out of nothing.

Why then are we poor? No one was born with money, all was taken out of the earth. You could also be the richest man from today. May God the giver, bless any person who will own one of this book for spiritual understanding of life to the glory of God.

CHAPTER FIVE

The Father, The Son, The Holy Spirit (The Trinity)

Gen. 1:26. Then God said, Let us make a man in our image, according to our likeness, and let them have dominion over the fishes of the sea and over the birds of the air, over the cattle, over all the earth, and over all creeping things that creep on the earth.

The word **OUR** in the above verse signifies that God is not alone but more than single entity. This confirms the Trinity. God is saying here that He is three entities in one and He and the other two entities are in agreement to make man in their likeness as stated in Gen. 1:26, 1John 5:7, and also in John 14:7 If ye know me ye should know my father, hence ye know him and ye have seen him

Hence God consist of:

The Holy Ghost	The Father	The son
the spirit	the soul	the body
[the unseen, having all	[The mighty, which dwells in	[The physical aspect of God,
power, and a great light	unapproachable light,]	the seen God, Expression
the mighty fire, the	Exo. 33:20	of the father manifested,
operator of God		producer, the vocal, and the power]

Hebr. 1:8. But unto the son he said Thy throne, Oh God forever and Ever. Amen. So Christ is God. Man is the representation of the trinity. The father is in the Holy Spirit, and the Holy Spirit in Jesus Christ. Christ is the physical aspect of God the father. God the father is the power, the soul of the unique God, and the three are one as:

THE TRINITY. **1 John 5:7** "For there are three that bear record in Heaven, *the father*, *the Word*, and *the Holy Ghost*: and these *three* are *One.*"

Gen. 1:27. "So God created man in his own image, in the image of God he created him, male and female he created them." God now becomes single in this verse. So God is three in one. The TRINITY. The word **HIS**, simply proves that the three are one, because the word **our** was no more used so God is three in one. Exo. 3:14. God said to Moses, I AM WHO I AM. This is what you are to say to the Israelites: I AM, has sent me to you. John 8:58. I tell you the truth, Jesus answered, before Abraham I AM. Hence the three are I AM. Therefore the man being the image of God, being created with all the qualities of God has the Body as Christ - [the body loves the world, and between God and Satan which is exposed to all the worldly influences-Pleasures, wealth, worldly joy, hardships and oscillation actions of life, reveals the father to the world, the grace unto mankind.] Soul as the Father - [the soul communicates with the father, purified from sin, the only sin that enters the soul is fornication and murder, only the originator commands and instruct the spirit. When the spirit is killed the soul has no strength but just support the body and has short life span.] Spirit as the Holy Ghost - [the action maker who uses the body for all instructions from the soul. Sin kills the spirit.] So the theory of man being the image of the three, God the Father, the creator is perfectly proven.

THE SOUL COMPONENTS:

1. The mind - the intellect [memory, reasoning, creativity.]
2. The emotion- feeling [desire, concern.]
3. The Will - the ability [responsibility.]

The soul is the spiritual principle embodied in human being, the real man which is immaterial. The soul is the storage house of the body. Whatever you do, either good or evil is recorded in. The soul makes you reason, because it has the mental body, the intellect. It makes you think and be creative. It is the soul that makes you feel - pain, when hurt and burn. It gives you desire, a taste for earthly things as well as spiritual things. You become concern about something by the soul's emotional body. The soul supplies the ability to do something. If the soul refuses to respond, your ability to create, to invent, to study and to memorize will be impaired. But the soul itself does not act even though he has all these qualities. The soul is always spiritual. He is always in contact with God. His contact with God will come to reality only when we convert the vocal to the body from the spirit, then we become magnificent to give glory to the father in all our deeds because the father created us for his glory. If one of the entities is lost eg. the spirit, the soul will still be performing his normal functions but without the spirit, the body becomes paralyzed or lost of senses [palsy or Alzheimer]. It's the result of lack of the word of God. Isaiah 43: 7. Everyone who is called by my name I have created him for my glory, whom I formed and make.

THE SPIRIT: The spirit is beyond the scope of human understanding, He is the possessor of the being. The spirit is the fusibility giving force, the sacred force which communicates with the soul. The spirit enable the human to think, walk, act, memorize, to see, in short to have the qualities of humanity. The spirit allows the man to live consciously when is properly cared for. He is left in an unconscious state when is not properly care for, where the person cannot differentiate evil and good. Evil becomes as good. Godly understanding is lost. In theological sense the spirit is called light so the light is quenched. This light is light from God. So Jesus said when I go I will send this light to you, he will help you and remember you of whatever I have told you. John 1:4-5. In him was life and the life was the light of men and the light shines in darkness and the darkness comprehend it not. It is the spirit which takes action. Without the spirit nothing will be achieved. This spirit is not the Holy Spirit but our intimacy with God by confessing Jesus Christ, God sends His Holy Spirit which cleanses and purifies and brings about the fusibility with biological spirit. This Godly spirit is given by the Lord Jesus Christ to those who believe in him and love him. John 14:21,26,15. The spirit body is the body of Grace. It is the body by which we shall resurrect with. The spirit translates the command of the soul [the father] to the body [the son].

THE BODY: is the temple of the SOUL and the SPIRIT in which both dwell and function. Without the body these two cannot function and made active. It comprises of the tissues and organs (flesh, heart, lungs, intestines, brain, lever, kidneys, etc.), and the water (two part hydrogen and one part of oxygen - and make about 80 to 90 percent of the human body), and the blood (platelet-which prevent hemorrhage; the plasma-mixture of water, protein, mineral; white cell - for the body defense; red cell - the oxygen transporter and the blood vessel - which contains the blood networking). The body is an essential part of the human and represents Jesus Christ.

The whole human system functions like a car:

1. The human physical body - - = The car body
2. The soul body---= The engine
3. The spirit Body---= The operator

The car body contains the engine and the operator. The engine does not operate the car. Someone must be at the control panel to control the vehicle. The spirit puts the power supply into work.

Most people usually do not see the value of their gift in them until it's presence is lost. The Lord Jesus said, you will not see the value of this light in your mist but if I go away then I will come in the form of the spirit to you and this is the one who does the fire works, He knows all things and capable of all works. The physical body is destroying the spirit, we feed the physical body and neglect the spirit body so the spirit body becomes powerless. We care more for the body than the spirit. Neglecting things like fasting, prayer and meditation means neglecting the spirit which is the operator of the being, therefore we only grow in the physical body and the spirit made retarded. Eating too much and physical desires are abuse to the spirit so you cleave to lust of the eye, the lust of the flesh and pride of life (1John 2:16). Feed the spirit and you will have good body. Negativity, evil thoughts, depression etc. make you spiritually impaired. When you are intuitively off balance, it means you are too physical. Know that your physical being is not the real you. The appearance we see as a man, is created with the composition of:

1. The Body
2. The Soul
3. The Spirit

So is God also, because God created the man in his own image and God is made up of

1. God the Father
2. God the Son
3. God the Holy Ghost

So man is a child of God, and is God the Child, as our Lord Jesus said in:

John 10:34. "Jesus answered, Is it not written in your Law I have said, You Are Gods, to whom the word of God came, and the scripture cannot be broken." and David also said: **Psalm 82:6** "I said, You are "gods"; you are all sons of the Most High.: But man has belittled himself and abused himself with sinful acts which had made him lost the godly quality in him, filled with earthly desires. A person learns to become supreme through positive prayers, positive meditation, positive fasting, proper exercise, healthy dieting, being self encouraged, not egoistic, charitable, being waiting always upon the Lord, and remembering to submit to the Lord your maker, **Matthew 22:37** Love the Lord your God with all your heart and with all your soul and with all your mind. When we give our love to God in Christ we shall receive back our lost spirit in Christ Jesus. Let us leave the physical body and cleave on the spirit. Because the scripture says we shall rise with a new body which is not this physical body so we must begin to practice to leave this physical body. All the power is stored in Christ and Christ has made provision for us to tap but it is up to us to make the effort to tap this power. **Luke. 10:17-19** "The seventy returned with joy and said, Lord even the demons submit to us in your name. He replied I saw Satan fell like lighting from Heaven. I have given you authority to trample on snakes and scorpions and to overcome all the power of the enemy; nothing will harm you. THE FATHER: is the soul, the mighty, who dwells in unapproachable light. THE SON: is the body, the physical aspect of God, the seen God, expression of the father manifested, the producer, the vocal and the power. THE HOLY GHOST: the spirit, the unseen, having all power and a great light, the mighty fire, the operator of God. We are the image of the three in- one God. In conclusion man being the image of God, soul, spirit and body has the qualities of God in him and for those qualities to function must draw near to God.

THE LORD'S SUPER

Memory scriptures Matthew 26:26-30; John 6:53-58;

Luke 22:15-20; 1Cor. 11:24-30; Exo. 12:20-24

Introduction: The pass over is a type of deliverance of the slavery being symbolized with the consecration of blood of animals (the blood of the first born of the Egyptians was used to sanctify the first born of the Israelites). That was the Passover of the night when the Lord passed through the land of Egypt but the new testament pass over is what we deserve for our sins to be washed with blood of Jesus Christ as has been applied to us by faith. The pass over would have been senseless and waste if the remnant was not consumed, likewise the blood of Jesus applied on the cross and His body consumed into the grave. So by the sacrifice of Our Lord and Savior Jesus Christ we are made to live by faith. The pass over was eaten with bitter herbs, as the bible says, eating the bitter herbs was not easy. What is bitter is bitter and it takes courage to eat in Exodus 12:12-14. Likewise the bitter herb represents public confession. For someone to abandon his old character is not easy. Jesus told the rich man, Go and sell your properties and share to the poor, abandon the old character or lifestyle and come to take this new character or lifestyle by following Me, and the man could not. Jesus said it is easy for the camel to pass through the eye of the needle than for a rich man to enter the kingdom of God. Matt. 19:24 That's what it takes for repentance by public confession, but that is the only means to seek for the kingdom of God. (Notice that none of the Israelites was consumed by the pass over) because they obeyed by eating the bitter herbs with the meat and applying the blood on their door frames. If we obey and come to Christ and repent and make public confession of our sins, we are saved and absolved into the kingdom of Christ. And finally participate in the Lord's super. The Passover and the Lord's Super are the same. The feast of unleavened bread came about when the Israelites were instructed to get ready to leave Egypt. They had no time to bake the normal bread but bread which did not stay overnight to gain volume and it became skim bread which is unleavened bread and it became part of the tradition of the Israelites to have the feast of the unleavened bread.

Meaning: The Lords Super is the central act of the faith given to Christians by Jesus Christ Himself. It is an act to remind the Christian of his or her position in Jesus Christ, making personal examination before the participation. If we eat and drink this cup in a sinful manner we eat and drink judgment to ourselves, without thinking of the holiness of Jesus Christ. Therefore we will have no judgment if we first judge ourselves. He who judges himself is not judged. The Lord's Super symbolizes the remembrance of Jesus Christ's suffering, His death and the great love He had shown to the world Hence it will not just become Christian tradition but a Christian purpose to focus on and the sacrament to help us strengthen our faith. The PASSOVER is the same as 1. THE LORD'S SUPER, 2. THE LAST SUPER, 3. COMMUNION. 4. EUCHARIST [thanking God for the work of Jesus Christ's sacrifice].

Institution: It was instituted in the night when Jesus Christ and His disciples met together to eat the Passover and Dr. Luke explains, that took effect on Thursday night. This shows that as the Passover was instituted in the old testament in the night when the Lord passed through the land, Even so, in the new testament the Lord Super was instituted the night Jesus commanded the disciples to go and prepare a place for the Passover (which is the feast of unleavened bread), in Matt. 26:17-20" Now on the first day of the feast of unleavened bread the disciples came to Jesus saying to Him, where do you want us to prepare for you to eat the Passover? And He said go into the city to a certain man and say to him, The Teacher says, My time is at hand. I will keep the Passover at your house with My disciples. So the disciples did as Jesus has directed them and they prepared the Passover. When even had come He sat down with the twelve." The Passover and the Lord's Super are the same. Even though it was there by name as Passover at the time of Moses, it was being celebrated once a year, but The Lord came to fulfilled that anytime the Christian congregation met they should celebrate it as a remembrance of Him Luke 22:19

The Importance Of The Lord's Super To The Christian.

The Lord's Super reminds us of the great sacrifice Our Lord Jesus Christ offered for our sake, His suffering before the Cross and that on the cross, which originally pertain to us. By faith the Lord's Super becomes sacred meal possessing healing power. When we celebrate the Lord's Super, we are expressing our gratitude to God for His mercy and His acceptance of us for this new relationship as being part of the body of Our Lord Jesus Christ. The Lord's Super connects us to Jesus Christ as long as we keep celebrating it. It is a symbolic celebration which Our Lord Jesus established for His remembrance to acknowledge our participation in the benefit of His death and fellowship with Him till He comes. 1Cor. 11:26.For whenever you eat this and drink this cup you proclaim the Lord's death until He comes.

The Lord's Super Replaces The Passover

The Passover was a feast which the Jewish people celebrate as a covenant with Jehovah for their deliverance from slavery of the children of Israel from Egypt. In this night a lamb was slaughtered and applied the blood on the door frames to separate the children of Israel from the Egyptians, which end up killing every first born in the land of Egypt. It is assumed as a symbolic deliverance of God's people from slavery. It was the time of celebrating the Passover that Jesus replaced with the Lord's Super. Luke 22:7-20

The Lord's Super as a covenant

The Lord's Super is in two parts, the bread which is the body of Jesus Christ and the wine which is the blood of Christ. Eating the bread which is the body of Jesus Christ gives us the opportunity to become part of the body of Christ, physically and spiritually and gives confidence in both realms. The wine which is the blood of Jesus is in some case called "the Cup" which had cleansed us of all our sins and totally forgiven and made us new creatures. 2Cor. 5:17. This is a new covenant Luke 22:20 by which we are assured that Christ will never forsake us, as long as we continue to celebrate this for His remembrance Luke 22:19; 1Cor. 11:25. This covenant is a legal agreement between Christ and us, and our relationship.

Who Should Participate in the Lord's Super?

The Lord's Super has no barrier of who should participate. The only qualification to participate is that the participant must be a Christian. You cannot participate in the Lord's Super and you do not know what you are doing. There are some warnings as to partake this celebration unworthy. It's for our benefit to heal us from our infirmities and intimate relationship with Jesus Christ and our connection with the Holy Spirit towards the second coming of Christ. If you operate a machine and you do not understand its functions, you can end up in terrible accident getting into being amputated and disable. Likewise the Lord's Super, if you eat and drink it without understanding what you're doing, you may eat and drink it unworthy which can end up with a curse. A curse go so much far to generations upon generations. So let's understand what we are doing and have the blessing. 1Cor. 11:29 "For he who eats and drink in an unworthy manner, eats and drinks judgment to himself not discerning the Lord's body." Someone will like to ask, how many time do we have to celebrate the Lord's Super? As often as we meet depending on the financial capacity of the church and availability and willingness to participate. 1Cor. 11:25

The Blessing Of The Lord's Super

We are sinners and were not qualified to celebrate the feast of the Lord's Super. It is just the grace of God that we also participate in this feast. As we participate we show our obedience and appreciation of Christ's sacrifice and God blesses us for our act of humility. With the celebration of the Lord's Super we are healed of our infirmities or sicknesses. So the blood of Jesus as we drink is a medicine without expiring date which has the potential to heal every disease tormenting the Christian. It is always a fresh and powerful medicine. This is a big guarantee and a breakthrough for the Christian.

ANGELS OUR CORPORATE PARTNERS

Angels are God's manifestations who are spirit beings. The corporate partners means they are at our disposal at any time. We are made to understand that every Christian has an angel before God Matt.18:10. "Take heed that you do not despise one of these little ones for I say to you that in heaven their angels always see the face of My father who is in heaven." The word angel was derived from the Greek word angelos which means intermediary, someone who correspondence between two media in otherwise a messenger.

Angels are spirit beings which communicate between man and God Matt.4:11. One cannot be messenger if he is not trustworthy, therefore an angel is a holy righteous being who protects and saves. Here we see the picture of CHRIST as the angel of God, who communicated the plan of God based upon His word and salvation towards mankind. Luke 19:10; Daniel 3:25. Angels are spirit beings which can transfigure depending upon the type of operation assigned to be accomplished. We see so many examples in the bible like, Jacob prevails over the angel Gen. 32:I, 24-30; Some strangers are angels Heb. 13:2: Gen.18:2; Gen. 19:10. Angels are celestial beings with human resemblance and for this matter they have the choice of human appearance and even remain human Gen. 6:2.

CHARACTER OF ANGELS:

1. Angels can be visible Gen. 18:1-2,19:1; John 20:12; Exo. 3:2-6
2. Angels are invisible 1Sam. 3:7-10; Gen. 22:11
3. Angels were created by God Psalm 8:5; Hebr. 1:6-7
4. Angels do not have their own will. Hebr. 1:13
5. Angel are sons of God. Luke 20:36; Gen. 6:2; Job 1:6
6. Angels have extremely high intellect 2Sam. 14:20; Mark 13:32; 1Peter 1:12
7. Angels Protect human Daniel 6:22
8. Angels are righteous and holy Luke 8:38

9. Angels have immeasurable strength. Psalm 103:20.
10. Angels do not marry Matt. 22:30

Angels have different categories of assignment. We have angels whose responsibility is to protect God in Heaven in otherwise they are the body guards. The same angels guarded the garden of Eden when the rightful owners abused their right and were rejected. They are the most powerful angels and they are the group of CHERUBIM. They carry wings which means they do fly and very fast in operation, no matter how long the distance, it takes second Gen. 3:24.

We have a second fast classification of angels who also carry wings and they protect the Throne of God in Heaven. They do not depart from the Throne and always proclaim the holiness of Our Father. These are known and called SERAPHIN Isaiah .6:1-3. Each of these celestial beings has six wings, three on each side [back of the left and right shoulders] which each pair represent one of these, obedience (worship), peace (praise and adoration) or, love (action) and that's their qualification for worship, a highly gifted celestial super worshipers. The second pair of the wings control respect among the angelic host apart from the Cherubim. They impact spirit of humility to all the angels and mankind. This shows that man is not of himself but for God. The last and third pair of the wings make them vanish, a movement more faster than any celestial beings or object in the universe. This tells us how fast they can respond to emergencies. Jesus said this is the doings of God and no one can understand it.

Third qualification of angels are the Archangels. They are the labor force of creation in heaven and they have exceedingly mighty power beyond expression, they also respond in time of war against the nation of God. They also protect the all the properties of God. They are seven in number, they are very swift, one can anticipate the imagination of their response. They are 1. Michael 2. Gabriel 3. Lucifer 4. Atziluth 5. Briah 6. Yetzirah 7. Assiah

1. Michael. The leader warrior and fighter. He is always for victory. He was the corporate partner of Israel's victories, Joshua 5:13-15

2. Gabriel. The messenger for principal communications for highly important messages and blessing. Luke 1:26-38

3. Lucifer. This name means the son of the morning in otherwise the light of God. We saw this in the creation. This is the angelic name for Satan prior to his fall. He is the fallen archangel. He was the intermediary of the Godhead bodily and the angelic host. He fell due to rebellion and power struggle which ended him all the satanic names as: 1. Satan Job 1:6; Luke 10:12, 4:10: Rev. 12:9 2. Dragon Rev. 12.9; 3. Devil. Rev.12: 9; Eze. 28:14: 4. Accuser Rev. 12:10: 5. The Old Serpent 2Cor. 11:3;. Oppressor Acts 10:38; 7. Liar and murderer John 8:44 7. Prince of the Air Eph. 2:2: 8. Prince of the Darkness Eph. 6:12: 9. Prince of the World John 12:13, 16:11: 10. God of this World 2Cor. 4:4: 11. The thief John 10:10: 12. The Roaring Lion 1Pet. 5:8: 13. Corruptor of Mind 14. Beelzebub Matt. 10:25. Every Christian knows the story of his fell and his jealous deeds against man on earth.

4. Atziluth. This is the angel in charge of the sight of creation. A powerful angel with unimaginable strength and divine intelligence. The bible says, and the earth had no form, and the spirit was hovering on the surface of the waters

5. Briah. The angel in charge of the world of thrones of the nations in the interest of the inhabitants of the nations when the people cry unto the Lord about the kings. 1. God creating the thrones of nation. God prepared a garden and placed man in it. God's name is in the angel and once you see His angel, you see His visitation. Adam did not pay attention to the voice of the angel.

6. Yetzirah. This angel is the God's anointing upon the creation and good things of nation and thrones.. And God saw that it was good. He is God's help for people of the nations to do the will of God by being obedient. This archangel work in conjunction with Archangel Assiah for the control of the heart of the inhabitants of nation to obey God.

There are the angels known as the Host Of Heaven who are always before the Father in heaven. There are given among those who believe and are followers of Christ. They show up with the form of Holy white Doves,

Intermediaries, Watchers [watching on Christians]. They can even take the form of humans. They are the sign of the appearance of the Holy Spirit. John 1:32-33.

There is the Guardian Angels which are the sole corporate partners who work hand in hand with the believer. They are the gift of God to the believer from the Holy Ghost ready to act or intervene at anytime in any operation or danger. We also plan and take decision from the Lord through them. They are intercessors. Matt. 18:10, Luke 9:55.

In conclusion angels are our corporate partners to work in agreement with us. So we can ask them for any help or dispatch them to go and perform specific operations based on the will of God, and they will obey and do. Matt. 8:8-9. We are not to worship them but they are to help us and to work with us in whatever we do.

RAPTURE

Matt. 24:35 Heaven and earth will pass away, but my word will by no means pass away. Matt. 24:36 But of that day and hour no one knows, not even angels of heaven, But the Father only. Isaiah 10:8 What will you do in the day of punishment and in the desolation which will come from afar? To whom will you flee for help and where will you leave your glory? Rev.14:13 Blessed are the dead who die in the Lord from now on. Yes, says the spirit that they may rest from their labors and their works follow them.

MEANING OF RAPTURE:- Rapture is the snatching of the Christ church in otherwise Christians or Christ congregation. In John 14:2-3 Christ gives Christians hope after death, quote "In my Father's house there are many mansions if it were not so I wouldn't have told you. And if I go and prepare a place for you, I will come again and receive you unto Myself, that where I am there you will be also. This is the assurance of the Christian, so that the Christian is not wasting his or her time, but preparing toward eternity which there is. The rapture is the departure of the followers of Christ from this earth as the bible has said from time to time as also in 1Thess. 4:16-17 "For the Father Himself will descend from heaven with a shout, with the voice of an archangel, and with the trumpet of God. And the dead in Christ will rise first. Then we who are alive and remain, shall be caught up together with them in the clouds to meet the Lord in the air. And thus we shall always be with the Lord. Therefore comfort one another with these words."

The rapture is the day of the Lord, It will come as a thief in the night, the sudden destruction which will come upon people at their time of their marrying- which will be equally like the labor pain upon a pregnant woman and nobody shall escape as said. Matt. 24:19, 43-44 "But woe to those who are pregnant and those who are nursing babies in those days" "But know this that if the master of the house had known what hour the thief would come, he would have watched and not allowed his house to be broken into. Therefore you also be ready, for the son of man is coming at an hour you do not expect." Those in the Lord spiritually and committed will not be overtaken as a thief in the night by this destruction, they are aware of it and they are prepared for it. Those of us who have heard of this, let us put on (i) the breast plate of faith and love and (2) the hope of salvation as helmet against the rapture being the day of the Lord.

This is not judgment but the cleanup for judgment. Judgment is not for the ungodly because the ungodly is already condemned as is said in John 3: 18 "But whoever does not believe in Jesus Christ is condemned already because he has not believed in the name of the only begotten Son of God." Then there rises a question, WHY CHRIST? (1) Because Christ was sacrificed for the sins of the world, therefore it is an obligation for every human being alive to believe in the name of the Son of God, Our Lord and Savior Jesus Christ. (2) Another reason for condemnation is that the world had lived in darkness for far too long but when the light came among them, they still love the darkness and they did not receive the light which is Lord Jesus Christ. (3) Man had borne the image and the characteristics of Satan for far too long and for the love of the things of Satan man refuse to cleave unto immorality but to stay in morality, like unto incorruptible to corruptible. There are some unbelievers who have been living righteous life and those people can have the mercy of God if they will repent and confess the name of Jesus Christ and believe the Son of God just the time.

BEFORE THE RAPTURE

Impersonation of Christ:- People will deceive others that they are Christ. There will be wars and rumors that the end has come. There will be earthquakes in various places, nation will rise against nation, there will be famine and pestilence. There will be tribulations and killing of Christians and hatred by all nations for Christ sake. Many will be offended, they will betray one another and hate one another. Many false prophets will arise and deceive many. There will be lawlessness and people's love will be cold, people will be discouraged and confused. Those who will endure to the end will be save. The gospel will be preached in all nations as a witness in all nations and the end will come. False Christ and false prophets will do great signs and wonders to deceive even the elect who are the chosen Christians.

There will be the Rejection of the Son of Man by this generation, Luke 17:25. There will be more celebrations and reviling and legalization of abominations. Luke 17:26-28.

ACTION OF MANKIND AT THE RAPTURE

Those in Judah (in the cities) will flee to the mountains, Those on house top (people will run to the roof of the skyscrapers and) will remain there and will not come down. Those in the fields will not be able to come home for clothes. The pregnant and the nursing mothers will be in great affliction because how will they run. We should pray that it is not going to be winter where the earth is covered with snow. Where do we go? Man will go through tribulation which has never happened in the world before. If those days are not shortened all who are not rapture will perish (we have to pray for the mercy of God that we may not follow the false Christ and false prophets and that those days are shortened. Mark 13:20. The prophecy of Noah seemed a dream and the people rejected and went about their business and that prophecy came to pass and people perished. Also the prophecy of Sodom where Lot dwelt, the citizens did all kind of evil and rejected whatever warning given to them and continued with those deeds and the whole city was wiped out with brimstone from heaven. Likewise the prophecy of the Rapture will come at a time we do not expect. Many have refused and rejected the Rapture, so it shall be a surprise to mankind.

THE BEGINNING OF RAPTURE

1. The Sun will be darkened and the Moon also will be darkened. Darkness will fill the Earth, the Stars will fall from Heaven. The power of Heaven will be shaken. This will be for some days and not only one day. 2. The Elect will be gathered together from all the four corners of the earth. 3. The parable of the fig tree: when these things come then know that the time is near at the door Luke 13:6-9, (the churches will not bear fruit but filled with sin and the Lord will wish to cut them off and Angel have been pleading for one more chance.) 4. Rejection of the Son of Man and His suffering, Luke 17:25.

THE POWER IN THE BLOOD OF JESUS CHRIST

All in the history of Israel, forgiveness of sin requires blood sacrifice. Blood sacrifice is considered as a way of deliverance for mankind and also for a nation. Nothing was considered purified without the mark of shed blood of animal. Even until now, in certain parts of the world where voodoo is practiced, annual blood sacrifice is still being used as sin offering to consecrate humans and properties.

Leviticus 17:11. For the life of the flesh is in the blood, and I have given it to you upon the altar to make atonement for your souls: for it is the blood that makes atonement for the soul.

The blood represents the life force of the living soul. The eating of blood was strictly prohibited in the kingdom of children of God, and the following bible verses confirm it:

Gen. 9:4-6. "But you shall not eat the flesh with its life, that is, its blood. Surely for your lifeblood I will demand a reckoning; from the hand of every beast I will require it, and from the hand of man. From the hand of every man's brother I will require the life of man. Whoever sheds man's blood, By man his blood shall be shed; For in the image of God He made man."

Leviticus 17:13-14." Whatever man of the children of Israel, or of the stranger who dwell among you. who hunts and catches any animal or bird that may be eaten, he shall pour out its blood and cover it with dust; for it is the life of all flesh. Its blood sustains its life. Therefore I said to the children of Israel. You shall not eat the blood of any flesh, for the life of all flesh is its blood. Whoever eats it shall be cut off."

In pagan worship the drinking of blood was incorporated into ritual practice where the participant was believed to have captured the life force of the creature by eating it's blood. **Hebr. 9:22** "And according to the law almost all things are purified with blood and without shedding of blood there is no remission."

Because when Moses had spoken and laid down the principle intentions of the agreement to all the people according to the law, he took the blood of calves and goats with water, scarlet wool and hyssop and sprinkled both the people, the books, the alter, almost everything pertaining to divinity in the tabernacle and the tabernacle for a complete atonement and all was considered to be sanctified and holy. Also the bible says in **Exodus 16:16** "So he shall make atonement for the Holy Place, because of the uncleanness of the children of Israel, and because of their transgressions, for their sins; and so he shall do for the tabernacle of meeting which remains among them in the mist of their uncleanness." The atonement was casual intersession of deliverance which never took away ones transgressions completely. It was a way which was provided out of His love for the sake of the people. With all the rebellion God did not abandoned man, He continued to seek for our welfare to communicate with Him. But in this new testament era the animal blood sacrifice for the sin of mankind has no value and does not valid, because the bible says in **Romans 3:23** "All have sinned and come short of the glory of God. Therefore it is not this our modest sins that make us come short of God's glory but the sin by which we are born." **Romans 5:12.**" Therefore just as through one man sin entered the world and death through sin and thus death spread to all men because all sinned". And again **Romans 5:18**. "Therefore, as through one man's offense judgment came to all men, resulting in condemnation, even so through One man's righteous act the free gift came to all men, resulting in justification of life." So we see that we are justify by the shedding of the blood of Jesus Christ being the eternal purpose of God. The bible says in **Luke 22:43-44** "An angel came from heaven and strengthened Him whilst He was in agony and prayed earnestly and His sweat became like great drops of blood falling down to the ground." This shows us to know that Jesus began shedding His blood for the redemption of the world at the time of prayer before they arrested Him. The crucifixion started from the time of prayer before He made the final completion of settlement on the cross. This mean, it was not human beings who shed His blood for the great mission on the cross but He gave it up at His own will on the cross. The sacrifice of Christ was not the plan of man, and for this, Pilate sought for a way to release Jesus. He even sent Jesus to Herod so he can take advantage of Herod's judgment but that did not work for him. The people intensified their cry that crucify Him! crucify Him! "Let His blood be on us and our children" **Matt. 27:25,** this is just another way of saying, how can we have salvation if you let this man go. And that made Pilate to give Him up to be crucified so that the scripture might be fulfilled. If what the scripture has said did not come to pass, there wouldn't have been any salvation, but this is the doings of the Lord. Therefore **Hebr. 9:12-14** says "Neither by the blood of goats and calves but by His own blood He entered in the holy place having obtained eternal redemption for us. For if the blood of bulls and of goats and ashes of heifer sprinkling the uncleaned, sanctifies to the purifying of the flesh. How much more shall the blood of Christ who through the eternal spirit offered Himself without spot to God purge your conscience from dead works to serve the Living God."

1Peter 1:3,18,19 "Bless be the God and Father of our Lord Jesus Christ which according to this abundant mercy hath gotten us again into a lively hope by the resurrection of Jesus Christ from the dead." Knowing that you were not redeemed with corruptible things like silver or gold from your aimless conduct received by tradition from your fathers. But with the precious blood of Christ as of a lamb without blemish and without spot.

1John 1:7 "But if we walk in the light, as He is in the light, we have fellowship with one another, and the blood of Jesus Christ His son cleanses us from all sin."

Gala. 3:10 "For as many as are of the works of the law are under the curse for it is written, curse is everyone who does not continue in all things which are written in the book of the law to do it." Because we do not do all that is written in the book of the Law, our judgment was the curse of the cross but for God so loved us He gave His only begotten Son that as we believe in Him we will not perish but have an everlasting life and Jesus was sent to the cross in our stead. Since Jesus went to the cross, It has not been heard or read, anybody has been executed by the cross. Those two criminal with Jesus were sentenced ahead of Jesus.

Eph 1:7 "In whom we have redemption through His blood, the forgiveness of sins according to the riches of His grace." He has brought us out of captivity, as the Israelites were brought out of Egypt. We were in the kingdom of Satan practicing all kinds of moralities and having nothing to do with what was written in the book of the law and for this we were under curse but now we are redeemed.

Col. 1:20 "And having made peace through the blood of His cross by Him to reconcile all things unto Himself, by Him I say whether they be things in the air or in heaven." By one man, Jesus Christ, the whole world has been redeemed, and those sins will not be imputed against us. Once anyone accept Jesus Christ as his savior and Lord he is made free, the past is over.

1John 2:2 "And He Himself is the propitiation for our sins, and not for ours only but also for the whole world." So this is the greatest miracle in the history of the world that one man's blood has saved the whole world given the chance to receive salvation by confessing the name of Jesus Christ. This is the blood that heals your diseases, the blood which is the medicine without expiring date which has the miraculous potential to heal every disease by faith. There are two weapons given to the Christian for his welfare, [1] the blood of Jesus Christ which heals all our diseases and [2] the name of Jesus which make every prayer possible.

CHAPTER SIX

THE HOLY BIBLE

The word BIBLE means – Basic Instruction Before Leaving Earth.

The word HOLY means -- He Only Loves You.

Therefore because He, Jesus loves you, you must be able to acquire his basic instruction and apply them before leaving this material earth, to enable you to have a better accountability. Judgment is the final application to come upon man before the final destination. In otherwise Holy Bible means He Only Loves You For The Basic Instruction Before Leaving Earth, meaning all are required to know the bible. The bible is the name given to a revelation in a study containing different books compiled and bind into a single book.. The bible means book. A word derived from a Greek word "LA BIBLA." This bible is the one we call the "THE HOLY BIBLE." The bible is a complete library and encompasses all the revelations and books of the spirit and the living. It is the word of God, full of grace and full of truth, and the bread of life, sent from above for a sacrifice unto salvation. In some case the bible is referred to as:-

1. The scripture - the recorded spoken word of God
2. The Oracle - the spoken word of God
3. The word - the voice of God;
4. the testament - testimonies and revelation.
5. Covenant - agreement for salvation between God and man.
6. The Law - the spoken order or command from God.

The bible is made of two parts namely:-

1. the old testament - the mosaic and prophetic covenant.
2. the new testament - the new covenant.

The bible contains 66 books.

39 books of the old testament. The old testament is divided into four parts:-

1. Genesis to Deuteronomy - is the Law known as Pentateuch which is the five books of Moses.

[The Pentateuch is the instruction according to the time- communiqué.] There is confusion about the books Moses wrote. We have been hearing of six and seven book of Moses and eight, nine, and ten books of Moses, there is nothing like that, Moses wrote only five books, the rest are occult made books, imagined, formulated and written to suit their own occult purposes. As a Christian if you read those books you can be possessed and your salvation will be useless and meaningless.

2. Joshua to Esther - History;
3. Job to Song of songs - Poetry [poems];
4. Isaiah to Malachi - Prophets [prophecies].

The new testament contains 27 books.

They are from Matthew to Revelations. They are also divided into four parts namely:-

1. Matthew to John - Gospel [autobiography of Jesus Christ.
2. Acts - History [the acts of the apostles]
3. Romans to Jude - Epistle [correspondence - Laws - the communiqué.]
4. Revelation - Apocalypse [the prophecies]

THE BOOKS OF THE BIBLE AND THE AUTHORS

THE OLD TESTAMENT

1. 1 Genesis - Moses;
2. Exodus - Moses;
3. Leviticus - Moses;
4. Numbers - Moses;
5. Deuteronomy – Moses;
6. Joshua – Joshua;
7. Judges – Samuel;
8. Ruth – Samuel;

9. 1Samuel – Samuel;
10. 2Samuel – Nathan;
11. 1Kings –Jeremiah;
12. 2Kings – Jeremiah;
13. 1Chronicles – Ezra;
14. 2Chronicles – Ezra;
15. Ezra – Ezra;
16. Nehemiah – Nehemiah;
17. Esther – Unknown (but some say Ezra);
18. Job – Job;
19. Psalms – David;
20. Proverbs – Solomon;
21. Ecclesiastes – Solomon;
22. Songs of Songs – Solomon;
23. Isaiah – Isaiah;
24. Jeremiah – Jeremiah;
25. Lamentations – Jeremiah;
26. Ezekiel – Ezekiel;
27. Daniel – Daniel;
28. Hosea – Hosea;
29. Joel - Joel;
30. Amos - Amos;
31. Obadiah - Obadiah;
32. Jonah - Jonah;
33. Micah - Micah;
34. 34.Nahum - Nahum;
35. Habakkuk - Habakkuk;
36. Zephaniah - Zephaniah;
37. Haggai - Haggai;
38. Zechariah -Zechariah;
39. Malachi - Malachi

THE NEW TESTAMENT

1. Matthew - Matthew;
2. Mark - Mark;

3. Luke - Luke;
4. John –John;
5. Acts – Luke;
6. Romans - Paul;
7. 1Corintians – Paul;
8. 2Corintians – Paul;
9. Galatians - Paul;
10. Ephesians – Paul;
11. Philippians- Paul;
12. Colossians- Paul;
13. 1Thesselonians - Paul;
14. 2Thesselonians - Paul;
15. 1Timothy – Paul;
16. 2 Timothy – Paul;
17. Titus - Paul;
18. Philemon - Paul;
19. Hebrews - Paul;
20. James - James;
21. 1Peter – Peter;
22. 2Peter – Peter;
23. 1John – John;
24. 2John – John;
25. 3John – John;
26. Jude – Jude;
27. Revelation - John

Matthew 5:17:- Think not that I am come to destroy the law or the prophets: I am not come to destroy but to Fulfilled. So we see that the new testament and the old testament are identical: both have history, prophecy, Laws, and poetry. The new testament did not condemn the old testament but rather made it Complete. So the bible say you cannot add nothing and you cannot take out anything.

The bible is filled with all the subjects of the world. Eg.

1. **Medicine** - King Hezekiah was sick unto death and he was given medicine to heal. 2Kings20:7

King Asa disconnected from God and connected with physicians 2Chro.16:12

2. **Engineering** - King Uzziah built war machines 2Chro. 26:14-15 - Bezaleel molding of gold and silver cutting of stones and calving of timber. Exo. 31:1-5 Noah built the first ship Gen. 6:14
3. **Politics** - Jethro the father-in-law of Moses advises Moses to appoint ministers Exo. 18:13-27
4. **Management** - Planning - Luke 14:28-30
5. Science -the revelation of advancing and reversal of the day as a sign to Hezekiah by prophet Isaiah -2Kings 20:9 -11, scientific accuracy about marriage (the chemistry of love) -Matt. 19:4-6, 2Kings 4:34 Elisha stretches himself to keep the body of the dead boy warm to bring him back to life (transfer of body heat) the tender branches of the trees indicates that summer is near. Matt. 24:32, (agriculture).
6. **Accounting** - Jacob's counting of the flock -Gen. 30:31-32 Taking inventory and reporting
7. **Marketing** - Joseph sold to all nations -Gen.41:56-57
8. **Economics** - Joseph takes over Egyptian economy - Gen 41:39:40,48-49, made nation of Egypt rich.

So if you want to have a great education, consult the bible. Every verse of the holy bible has healing power, miraculous power and blessing for mankind.

THE BIBLE SLOGAN

This is my bible. It is the word of God. - John 1:1-5

Full of truth and full of grace - John 1:14

It is the bread of life - John 6:48

Sent from Heaven - John 6:29, 33, 38, 42

For a sacrifice unto salvation - John 19:15,18.

The bible is a book, written out of inspiration for every human being to study. It is the map of life. Life based upon the bible will never go into a ditch because the word BIBLE signifies BASIC, INSTRUCTION, BEFORE, LIFE, ENDS, It is the basic instruction for every being to abide by before he dies.

Breaking The Sin Curses Of The Past:-

BREAKING THE DEMONIC COVENANTS

Having been saved: there is more to be done for salvation as Christ like, that's Christian. In your past life the sins you committed, produced curses and those curses are those which possesses you- inscribed in your life. Even though our Lord Jesus Christ has forgiven you all your sins. Jesus has done His part, your sins are forgiven and cancelled but the curses of the sins produced in the past, it's your duty as a Christian, a Christ like, a child of God to work on your deliverance by

1. Fasting
2. Reading the Scripture
3. Prayer -: breaking of the curses - with the blood and name of Jesus, and the power and the anointing of the Holy Spirit.

. In Zech 3:1-7 Satan remembered the past of Joshua and used it as legal ground to oppose him. It was the Lord who rebuked him, and liberated Joshua according to his works. Once you are saved you need to break the curses of the past. If a thief had a cut in the process of stealing and healed, the scar remains, he does not get rid of the scar by being forgiven the crime. Even though the sin of stealing is forgiven the scar will be there until he treats it by applying dermatological creams to remove the scar which is the curses and is not easy to get rid of it. That's what you have to do as a Christian - breaking of the curses. Breaking is very important after being saved. You will call yourself a Christian but because of the sin curses you do not function as a Christian.

Why the curses? Because you have put people in pain and they have spoken curses out of bitterness into your life. Ancestral is the curse when our forefathers served idols and did evil in the sight of God and before man and we had inherited the curses. In like manner generational curses are your own evil and sinful deeds that had put people in pain and become a curse. These curses do not easily come out by salvation. Salvation is one thing and deliverance is also another thing.

This is the more reason why many Christians are suffering and things are not going well with them. We make Christ a liar, that's why when you speak about Christ to people they do not want to hear you, because they do not see your salvation. I have seen Christians being delivered and the curses in them manifest and tell their storey of the past. All is done by the same Christ who gave the same salvation. So after salvation you need to do the:-

1. Breaking of the curse of poverty.
2. Breaking of the curse of barrenness.
3. Breaking of the curse of impotency.
4. Breaking of parental and public curses of Child Abuse, child labor and slavery.
5. Breaking of the ancestral curses.
6. Breaking of the generational curses.
7. Breaking of the curse of rape.
8. Breaking of the curse of humiliation.
9. Breaking of the curse of oppression.
10. Breaking of the curse of sexual weakness.
11. Breaking of the curse of homosexuality that's gay and lesbianism.
12. Breaking of the curse of physical and mental illness, and masturbation.
13. Breaking of the curse of action limitation.
14. Breaking of the curse of CORRUPTION.
15. Breaking of the curse of infirmity.
16. Breaking of the curse of pride, jealousy, selfishness, greed, gluttony, sloth, Envy, Wrath and lust and many more. It is not possible to break all these in one day because they are powerful demons with great force using peoples past to destroy their future.
17. Breaking of the curses of kidney failure, heart failure, lungs, lever, in short organ failure. Curse is word spoken which becomes spirit and after many years begin to operate. An evil word or evil thought out of anger becomes a curse and a curse is a demon. You can imagine how many people have cursed you.

A man drown in a river but the rescue squad saved him. Because he made fun of a disable person, and the disable person told him, "he will perish by water, he will never be the same tomorrow." He took it as joke and did nothing about it, and after many days he drown in a river. He did not die, but he was sick the rest of his life till he died. That was the curse invoked upon him because what the disable person told him was a curse. Curse comes by words and deeds and this shows how powerful are words and our deeds.

In Zech. 3:1-7. Satan remembered the past of Joshua and used it as legal ground to oppose him. It was the Lord who rebuke him and the filthy garment on Joshua was removed. He was a great man of God but there was hindrance in his life which served as legal ground for Satan. This can happen to anybody.

Elisha was a regular person who lived normal life. He was a business man, a farmer, and was rich. And because of the work of God and Israel, he abandoned his business and all his wealth and became the servant of God. He went from Bethel and was met by young people who caused him pain and felt bitter, because they disrespected his office in God and using his situation to mock him, saying" go up you baldhead," Elisha pronounced a word against them and they were mauled by two female bears. 2Kings 2:23-24. Elisha spoke words and it became a curse against them, forty-two of them all died. Words and deeds are very powerful so be careful with your words and your deeds, they could become curse and torment someone, even your family.

Breaking simply means destroying the works of Satan in your life. That is to tear in pieces, in otherwise destroying the legal grounds which Satan is using against you. When someone curses you, be careful it could be legal ground for Satan to get you. Refuse and reject it and break it, if possible reverse it. The following scriptures teaches us how to battle the enemy and break every curse in our lives.

1John. 3:8. "He that committed sin is of the devil. For the devil sinneth from the beginning, for this purpose the son of God was manifested that he might destroy the works of the devil. So we are empowered to destroy the works of the devil by the name of Jesus Christ." We do destroy the plans of the devil in our lives by the following three weapons;

1. Binding:-Matt. 18:18 Assuredly, I say to you, whatever you bind on earth will be bound in heaven and whatever you loose on earth will be loosed in heaven. Matt. 16: 19 I will give you the keys of the kingdom of heaven, and whatever you bind on earth will be bound in heaven, and whatever you loose on earth will be loosed in heaven.

2. The blood and the name of Jesus Christ:- It is the blood and the name which does the miracle. It cleanses and destroy every works of Satan. Rev. 12:11 They overcame him with the blood of the Lamb and by the word of their testimony.

3. Bombing-shooting, stoning:- Deut21:21, Joshua7:25 Then all the men of his city shall stone him to death with stone so you shall put the evil from among you, and all Israel shall hear and fear. Joshua 7:25 And Joshua said, "why have you troubled us? The Lord will trouble you today." So all Israel stoned him with stones; and they burn them with fire after they had stone them with stones.

4. Fire of the Holy Ghost-2Kings 1:10-12, So Elijah answered and said to the captain of fifty, If I am a man of God, then let fire come down from heaven and consume you and your fifty men. And fire came from heaven and consumed him and the fifty......; 1Kings 18:38, Then the fire of the Lord fell and consumed the burnt sacrifice, and the wood and the stones and the dust, and it licked up the water in the trench. 2Kings 6:17. And Elisha prayed and said, "Lord I pray, open his eyes that he may see." Then the Lord opened the eyes of the young man and he saw. And behold, the mountains was full of horses and chariots of fire all round Elisha. Luke 13:10-17. This woman was in the church sitting on the power in her as a child of God and yet crippled, she was in possession of the power to command the devil to leave but did not know how to use these weapons.eg. So many countries have all the mineral resources, but yet in poverty, why? Hosea 4:6, Isaiah 5:13

<u>Luke 9:54-55.</u> The disciples realized the power in them and were going to abuse it instead of using the power to perform miracles. So Jesus got mad with them and said even though you know that you have power, you do not have the knowledge of the kind of power you have. Knowledge is an essential factor in the life of every normal human being and in the growth of every economy. Therefore Jesus expected them to have the knowledge of humor, and not to destroy because that was not his mission in the world. NB.- Because they are poor in knowledge they cannot develop. You need knowledge to develop. Once you receive knowledge you can develop and as you develop you will acquire the riches of the land. Have you forgotten what Jesus did? He took your poverty that you shall be rich (2Cor.2:9). John 14:20. I am in my father, and ye in me and I in you. So the Holy Spirit, Christ, God the father and all angels are with you. If someone knows he hasn't what you have, he will do everything possible to cause you to loose the power you are blessed with, so he can possess it. When the priest heard the people said, what a power, they began to accuse the Lord Jesus for haven healed on the Sabbath. People will accuse you and speak evil of you just because they do not have the potentials and the gifts you are blessed with. So In Luke 13:10-17 They used the Sabbath as a yard stick against the Lord, not because he has done wrong, but it was because they were with the woman all her life and they did not have that knowledge that the woman was being tormented by Satan and also because they were not able to do what Jesus was capable to do. God does not want deformity, things that are deformed (Mala. 1:7-8) so beware and attack the devil and break the deformity. Poverty is a disease. It's deformity, a curse. There're two characteristics in the bible (Abraham, and Lazarus) God said I am the God of Abraham, Isaac and Jacob. God did not say I am the God of Lazarus. But God raised him from the dead. Poverty is not from God, God is full of unlimited riches and resources. There is no poverty in God but He love the poor and desire to change their status.

Phil. 4:13. I can do all things through Christ which strengthens me. Prayer, fasting, righteousness, and the Holy Ghost are the weapons. Jer. 51:20-24. We have the weapon to break all the plans and deeds of Satan. Like Illness, poverty, spiritual marriages, marriage breakdown, all form of deformity. What do you do with the power you now posses? The Lord Christ Jesus

has invested power in you. It is a sin not to use this power so now begin to use this power and enjoy that investment that the Lord has made in you. The power is yours to utilize it.

Curse causes dilapidation, it causes desolation, when we refuse to obey God, we attract curse. Galatians 3:10 For as many as are of the works of the law are under the curse, for it is written, curse is everyone who does not continue in all things which are written in the book of the law, to do them. Again:

Malachi 3:9 "You are curse with a curse, for you have robbed Me, even this whole nation." there is no sin that man will commit and freely walk away. All come with a curse.

Abraham lied; Gen. 12:13, Gen. 20:2 and the effect affected his descendants. They became slaves in Egypt, a foreign land for forty years. Gen. 15:13-14 "Then He said to Abraham: Know certainly that your descendants will be strangers in a land that is not theirs and will serve them and they will afflict them for forty years. That nation that they serve, I will judge afterwards they shall come out with great possession." Slavery is a curse. So the curse came upon Abrahams descendants for forty years.

Isaac also lied; Gen. 26:7 and the Philistines had to opposed him when he prospered and move from one place to another, terrible distraction of his prosperity. Gen. 26: 12-21 "Isaac sowed in the land and reaped in the same year a hundred fold and the Lord blessed him. He began to prosper and continued prospering and became very prosperous. He had possession of flocks and great number of servants. The Philistines had stopped up all the wells which his father's servants dug in the days of Abraham his father and they had filled with earth." Being opposed is a curse, is the spirit or the curse of opposition, because it distract your progress and can render you poor- curse of poverty.

Jacob lied to claim the birthright and ended him in the house of his uncle, Laban, while running for his life. Gen. 27:18-30 "Jacob said to his father I am Esau your firstborn. I have done just as you told me. Please arise. sit and eat of my game that your soul may bless me." Jacob had to run for his life spirit of distress and fear and affliction and oppression were all after Jacob and became homeless, a curse which has to be dealt with but God love him because he was obedient to God.

Joseph felt superior to his brothers because his mother was the legitimate wife (the wife his father wanted and the rest were impose on him) of Jacob his father. Bilhah and Zilphah were maids who became wives. For this Joseph was proud. Gen. 37:2-4 Pride comes with a curse. He posed as supervisor over his brothers and was reporting them and nearly lost his life, he was sold and sent to Egypt. Gen. 37:2 "This is the history of Jacob. Joseph being seventeen years old was feeding the flock with his brothers. And the lad was with the sons of Bilhah and the sons of Zilphah his father's wives and Joseph brought report of them to his father." He was causing a sin that could cause division in the family which may result in chaos, he was sold and taken to a foreign land. Being a stranger in a foreign land is a curse but may also come with a blessing. Some curse end with blessing.

King David committed the worse crime by committing adultery with Bathsheba and finally killed the husband Uriah, 2Sam. 11:15, and married her. And King David's own son Absalom rose against him and nearly killed him. King David, the great warrior at that time had to run for his life. 2Sam. 11:4-5" David sent messengers and took Bathsheba and she came to him and he laid with her for she was cleansed from her impurity and she returned to her house. And the woman conceived, so she sent and told David and said I am with child." But King David was obedient to God. 1King 15:5 "King David did what was right in the eyes of the Lord and had not turn aside from anything that He commanded him all his life, except in the matter of Uriah the hittite." The curse put David in a threatening situation to run for his life and abandoned his throne and his glory. This shows how many people will abandon their riches when they see death and how threatening curse is.

Moses killed an Egyptian and run for his life. God worked miracles with him and did marvelous works with him but at the end he did not step foot on the promise land, only with his eyes he saw. Exo. 2:12 (11-14) "So he looked this way and that way and when he saw no one, he killed the Egyptian and hid him in the sand." To punish or to kill a person is the decision of God so if it becomes a human decision, it is sin and that was what Moses did. So Moses became homeless and a stranger in a foreign land but ended with a blessing as a great man of God.

King Solomon suffered from the generational curse of womanizing because his father was, 1Kings 11:1-4. Because of this generational curse King Solomon deviated from the way of his God, the God of Israel and worshipped idols and shrines through women. 1Kings11:6-7 "Solomon did evil in the sight of the Lord, and did not fully follow the Lord, as did his father David. Then Solomon built a high place for Che'mosh, the abomination of Mo'ab, on the hill that is east of Jerusalem, and for Mo'lech the abomination of the people of Am'mon." The house of Solomon lost their glory, the kingdom was taken from his descendants and they became ordinary people, that is the curse. Solomon love God and love idols like his great great grandfather, Terah the father of Abraham, for his name is still remembered.

In conclusion, sin is sin, great or small are equally the same, they are all sin and all come with curse, which take different form. Therefore man must be careful of sin and do everything possible to avoid sin. The curse may not manifest in the youthful age, and that is the most painful era of life. It may even go as far as the descendants, whereby they may not be able to trace the root of the curse. These people were descendants of Abraham, and they still enjoyed life and the glory because of the covenant God made with Abraham, but they were prayerful and break those curses in their lives. Our Lord Jesus Christ has given us the weapon and showed us how to break these curses and destroy the legal grounds being used by Satan against the children of the Living God. The weapon is breaking of the curses and commanding and declaring total destruction of them. One thing we have to know is curse is a spirit and should not be allowed to live. All these people, even though they went through terrible situations they never abandoned their God so at the end they were blessed. By the grace of Jesus Christ we now know how to deal with these curses.

WORD OF INSPIRATION

1. It is impossible to give in your lack but the possibility to give in your lack will take you out of your lack.
2. If you believe in lack, you will always be in lack. You can not violate this. Meditate on the word and it will manifest.
3. Nobody can stop you from reaching your future, only you can stop it. God has designed your future to put your enemies in pain. God wants to change you from inside out. All is possible through believing and meditation. It is time to get rid of the limitations on yourself, wake up and allow God to do His work.
4. Once you take things beyond your mind by prayer, the spirit will take it up. Prayer is spiritual issue. Prayer goes to the root of the problem. We do the praying and God does the work. Prayer means entering into God's bedroom and you need God's spirit to enter into His bedroom. Those who worship God worship in spirit and in truth.
5. Faith takes you bound if you are only dealing with the natural aspect of matters, then you will not achieve anything.
6. Anytime you deal with God, you have to deal with FAITH. You have to have physical to see the physical things likewise you have to have the spirit to see spiritual things. God has to come to the world in the physical to take care of the physical burden. Those who have both see deeper.
7. People are poor not because they do not have money. They are poor because they do not have the knowledge. Prosperity is not potential by race or color. People deal with the flesh but dealing with the spirit is the most powerful.
8. Expensive sacrifice will results in expensive breakthrough.
9. You have to experience poverty to manage blessing likewise you have to taste **tribulation** to manage freedom. Poverty is a curse and it takes a mighty power to break it. It could only be broken by the power of God, which is the hand of God, the blood and the name of Jesus Christ, the power and anointing of the Holy Spirit.

10. Tribulations and afflictions are the fountains of one's life because everyone desires breakthrough, whereas disappointments sometimes is used to strengthen us.

11. The principle of the world is seeing is believing but the principle of God is believing is seeing which is a contradiction between the old world and the new world.

12. How will you know the Most High God when you do not hear from Him. You have to hear from God to know Him.

13. Death is a temporally separation, and it means sleep. So when a Christian dies, he or she is asleep.

14. When the anointing of God is upon you and God is using you even demons will admire you. And people do not see your education neither your personality but what they see is the anointing. Anointing is the physical aspect of the Holy Ghost. And that's what people see.

15. Patience is bitter but its fruits are sweet and appetizing.

16. Discernment is a remarkable opportunity whilst waiting is a remarkable discernment.

17. As a child of God you must be strong in relationship with God, for the interesting thing about Christians is not the miracles we do perform but our intimate relationship we maintain with God.

18. You need an overflowing anointing that can break the mountains, that is the level of anointing you need as a man of God and this anointing is in different categories.

19. When you are **desperate for solution,** you will always be tempted and will become distracted which turns to affliction and becomes oppression and finally a demonic covenant.

20. As a Christ follower you always need to cover yourself with the blood of Jesus.

21. Prophesy is what God wants to perform in your life. Do not ignore prophesy. Prophesy is God's **thaught** about you. If you will live according to His will then it shall come to pass.

22. Prophesy dies when you refuse to accept it by faith. It is like accepting a pregnancy by faith, you will deliver a child unto your bosom, but if the pregnancy is aborted you may have no child.

Likewise prophecy will not tarry but shall come to pass if it is accepted by faith.

23. Christians depend upon God's Spirit to serve Him, but religious worshippers serve God by traditional laws, which is a religious form of worship. if you depend upon the religious act of worship, you will never see the glory of God

24. If you are open God can do more with you. Distance is not a barrier with God's move.

25. Parable is the unveiling truth of God's way of doing things and intentions in the life of man.

26. Covenant is a deal initiated by God, built on well divine time and sealed by an oath. God cannot get out of His covenant unless we fail to do our part. Once we play our part God is committed to honor His prosperity contract. Covenant is a spiritual contract and not a promise. It is an oath sworn to abide by the two parties, a binding agreement

27. If you refuse and reject to **sow seed in your life is equivalent to praying for poverty.** Spiritual men who do not do charity become poor. You need to engage in quality covenant with God. Only covenant people with God can live under the open windows of heaven. Sowing your substance will bring about reaping of your blessing. The farmer sows and reaps. So sow and reap according to your faith.

28. If you think having enough to eat and drink is prosperity, you may be deceiving yourself, that's **survival.** Prosperity is sharing your blessing with other people. That's others can see you and smile, come to you and become blessed. That's what we call prosperity. eg. **Oprah Winfrey** has to build an education complex in South Africa to improve the lives of thousands, worth over forty million dollars. When these people see her they embrace her as their mother. She is the mother of thousands, the mother of kings, presidents, doctors and engineers. John 12:24. Oprah's approach is the smartest way of liberating millions of people from the grip of poverty in the next twenty years forever.

29. You need to be empowered to prosper because someone that has a greater power is holding your prosperity whom you do not see, and

you will need the greatest power to overcome him. It is impossible to have financial blessing and prosper without empowerment (God's favor). Satan deceives people of the word of God. If you need to be free of lack then you need to be empowered. Anytime you borrow, it belittles the power of God in your lives. Habitual **Lack and borrowing** is a sign of poverty. It needs to be broken. Accepting to be poor means accepting to be dead. It is the dead which is poor. We are made rich but someone is sitting on it. 2Cor. 8:9. It can be done by the blood and the name of Jesus Christ, the hand of God that is word of God and the power and anointing of the Holy Spirit. **PROSPERITY EMPOWERMENT:-** 2Cor. 8:9; 3John 2; Deut. 26:12-15, 7:12-15; 2Cor. 9:8,10.

30. God knows before hand that we need financial resource for everything and God grants that. We must have money. **Money** is answer to many things but not everything. Our social life can only be catered for by financial empowerment. Money is good but the love of it is evil and sin. 1Tim. 6:7,10,17-18.

31. God created us with **the dignity** (respect) **to transcend** (to go beyond our limits). **Borrowing** is not sin, it is a short term relief but when it becomes a habit, it can lead to slavery and become a curse.

32. Each and everyone has an **unction** with God to be great, that is for you to be heard worldwide, but if you allow dream killers, if you give them the opportunity, they will kill that dream. That's the work of dream killers. They will put fear in you, they will fill you with confusion, they will put you under desperation, they will frustrate you, they will destroy your image and they will lie about you.

33. Where there is faith, there is impossibility made possible. Faith has no imitation. You can't fake the Holy Ghost. Faith arises from the heart according to the word of God. For faith to be consistent it must be based on something more stronger and more solid. Faith based on consistency is a terror and nightmare to the Satanic kingdom but in these era emotions and feelings has become the spiritual experience of many believers.

34. When you do not have **God's Spirit to serve Him,** is like you are serving an object. Depending on God's spirit to serve Him will reveal God's taught about you

35. Satan is the author of complains and keep people complaining to be under his captivity, unless they are destined to be delivered, they will remain captive.

36. Your achievements in terms of wealth and possession, takes Satan no time to destroy it. Hence you need God and faith in God to protect your achievements. Faith comes by the spirit and not of the flesh. Have faith in God, for you need not to be sick to die, it's God's decision. Without God, Satan can knock you down at anytime he wants.

37. We work by time and not by faith but we walk by faith and not by sight. A disconnection in faith is a break in God.

38. Embracing the word of God is the most effective instrument for change and prosperity.

39. For a Christian every day is a good morning, because God's mercies and compassion fail not, they are new every morning. Never say good night for good night is for the dead. Night means darkness and refers to the grave.

40. If you speak about Jesus without righteousness which is God's Spirit, it will be an abomination.

41. Without God's Spirit, God's opinion and God's plan about your faithfulness (praise worship, fasting prayer, and charity) will be useless, vague and destructive.

42. Devotion is the tool for reading the bible, a God's satisfying desire which your life depends on.

43. All religions claim to be the same because they all teach and explain life and death and life after death, but the claim of superiority makes their difference which cause division in humanity.

44. You cannot serve someone you do not know. Therefore you have to know God to serve Him. If you know that God is your creator and your life is in His hands and without him you cannot exist then you can serve Him with all perseverance.

45. If you serve God without His spirit, you will be serving a God you do not know, lifeless god, an object. If God does not accept

your prayer, Satan will accept your prayer. There are two powers, God and Satan. We are made spiritual by living in the word and the word living in us. Philosophies and theories of the word does not cause spirituality. The holy bible becomes history without depending on God's Spirit to teach it. As well the Holy Bible is a history book in the hands of an unbeliever and the ungodly.

46. Knowing the reason why you are a Christian and being determine to achieve Salvation, but some powerful force stands your way to oppose you. The Spirit of God is the power and without Him nothing works in the universe.

47. The word of God becomes a living weapon in the lips of the believer when he depends on God's Spirit. Words are like seed, when they surround a person for far too long, they will gain root and take him captive. Satan loves to demonize and put negative trade marks on people to hold them captive. Satan knows God has wonderful and gracious talent in people so he visits them with discouragement, fear and inferiority to overcome God's purpose to achieve his own plan. Satan does not fight against your current situation, he fights against your future. He always plans ahead.

48. You are saved by the blood of Jesus Christ, but your prosperity depend upon your deliverance from the blood covenant (murder), the Demonic covenant (witchcraft) and the Satanic covenant (shrines) of your ancestors and generation. That scar is in there, you need to work on it to erase it, to pave the way for prosperity.

49. Anything that has no change does not grow and anything that does not grow cannot develop. Development is change which is valuable component that brings quantity from quality. Therefore prosperity becomes an outcast where there is no change.

50. Bitterness escalates heart troubles and results in hatred. There are doors without protection in life and when they are opened Satan become possible.

51. The more you call the name of the enemy, the more you critisize the enemy, the more you advertise the name of the enemy, the popular he becomes and the more proud he is. Better do not even mention his name and let his name die.

52. COURAGE TO WITHSTAND CRITICISM:- **1.** If you fear criticism you cannot be a leader. **2.** If you fear criticism you cannot even marry, because at your wedding, you will be criticized. **3.** If you fear criticism you cannot qualify as a human being. We are the image of God, and if God is criticized, left alone image. **4.** Criticism shows your importance and your value but do not let the criticism prove that judgment to be your character.

53. SEVEN KEYS TO CHRISTIAN FAITH: **1.** Pray for vigorous body for evangelism. Do not let your selfish and prejudice turn you away from the work of God. It is the only means to break down your negative tendencies. **2.** If you want to free yourself from death and attain the supreme Eternal Life then you must awaken the Christ-In-You. John 14:17-21. **3.** Do not allow anyone to hinder your dedication to the great mission of spreading Christianity which will bring peace in this world and after. Remember, only by witnessing for the LORD JESUS CHRIST will your entire life be CROWNED with glory. Matt. 19:27-29. **4.** Never become a mere observer. If you do, you will never know even a fraction of the profound joy in Christ. Matt. 9:13 **5.** If your faith is weak, you will be overcome by your negative tendencies and will not see the joy in Christ. Matt. 21:21-22. **6.** If you have weak faith in Christ you will be influenced by your negative tendencies, and hold grudges against others, keeping yourself away from the world of faith in Christ. Because of the negative tendencies, you will be unable to perceive that which is valid or correct, and will feel resentment and make justifications to suit your own purpose. This is the tendency, a tragic one of people whose faith is weak and eventually they backslide in their faith in Christ and extinguish the light which Christ has lit in them. Matt. 12:1-12; 2 Cor.12: 1-6 **7.** The benefit of the HOLY SPIRIT is mostly inconspicuous and as common mortals we tend to be always making short sighted judgment. So as a result even if one's prayer is not answered immediately, one will eventually find himself moving a positive direction towards benefits. There is profound meaning behind the fact that sometimes one's prayer seems to go unanswered. Hebr. 3:7-8

54. EVOLUTION: Even though people think of evolution as an independent operating faculty being the source of creation and its development, evolution itself must have source. And the source is God, who is the creator of this universe we live in. Because the bible says in Rom. 1:20 "For since the creation of the world, His invisible attributes are clearly seen being understood by the things that are made, even His eternal power and Godhead so that they are without excuse." So there is no excuse whatsoever on earth for a human being to say there is no God or I do not believe in God. Job 9:24 says, "The earth is given into the hand of the wicked. He covers the faces of its judges. If it is not He, who else could it be." Now we see how evolution believers are deceived by the devil. They have allowed themselves to be blinded by the demon of evolution, making them to understand that there is no God who created the universe. These are some supporting scripture quotations. Psalm 14:1; 2Cor. 4:4; John 12:40; Matt. 13:14-15; Hosea4:1-3,6.

55. ACCEPTING CHRIST: One accept out of the power of miracle unto the power of faith, then out of the power of faith repentance is made unto forgiveness to salvation. It is easy to accept, but difficult to continue but continuing faith in Christ leads to ETERNAL LIFE.

Why Smoking Cigarette

Smoking is sin in the house of God (the Lord). Because the bible says the body is the temple of God, and the temple of God is where the angels of God and the Spirit of God dwell. So when you smoke, you drive the spirit of God and the angels of God away or suffocate them to evacuate them out of the temple. The man who smokes, he brings toxic chemical into the temple of God, that's the body, to kill the angels of God and the Holy Spirit. So the smoker is a killer and a criminal because smoking is a crime. Every criminal is liable for judgment and liable for punishment.

CHEMISTRY OF CIGARETTE SMOKE

Scientist have found that Cigarette Smoke contain nicotine, carbon monoxide, carbon dioxide, nitrate methane, nitrogen dioxide, hydrogen sulphide, carcinogenic (tars), methyl alcohol, glycerine, glyco (alcohol and esters), acetaldehyde, acroliein, acetone, prussic acid, carboxyle derivatives (acids), chrysene, nicotrosamines (alkaloids), cresols (phenols), radioactive compounds (nickel, polonium, plutonium), hydrocarbon (benzopyrene, benzene, isoprene, toluene, arsenic, cadmium, naphthylamines. This is the chemistry of cigarette smoke which are dangerous chemicals. They are all dangerous toxics. It has been found by scientist and medical doctors that the tars (**carcinogenic**) in the cigarette smoke create a film deposit on the walls of the respiratory tract and the lungs and cause them change color to become black and is the cause of many lung cancer diseases. If a smoker smokes a pack of cigarette per day, it's equivalent to a small beer glass of tar per year, into the lungs which may also sum up to 225 gr. on average. Carbon monoxide (Co) is an asphyxiating gas which is normally produced by car exhaust fumes which is 1.5% of the composition of the fume. That of cigarette is said to be higher than that of the car which is 3.2% of carbon monoxide and slowly asphyxiates the blood and needs twelve to twenty-four hours to dissipate. **Nicotine** is a powerful insecticide and poisonous for the nervous system which also **cause addiction, a demonic chemical**. According to scientists, four sticks of cigarette contain fifty milligrams of **nicotine** which is enough to kill a man if used as an injection into the blood stream. The **nicotine** is diluted in the smoke which take a short time to reach the brain, stimulates the brain cells and block the nervous impulse and cause addiction. **Nicotine** speeds up heart rate and cause contracting and hardening of the arteries, the heart then pumps more and receives little blood putting the heart in a terrible labor or over work.

POLITICS ON CIGARETTE

No Government will allow his citizens to smoke but for the sake to maintain the factory and the workers and the taxes, governments encourage the existence of the cigarette factory. For this Jesus has cause governments to provide a law against smoking. On every pack of cigarette it is written: DANGEROUS TO YOUR HEALTH; WHICH MEANS YOU DON'T HAVE TO SMOKE AND THE SMOKER IS LIABLE FOR PUNISHMENT, WHICH COULD BE SPIRITUAL, and we see smokers getting terrible illness. Smoking is committing a slow suicide, and committing suicide is a crime. Cigarette smoking is not good for our health. Someone may say Why? and this alone is not enough. Cigarette is obtain from tobacco with little amount of nicotine added to it which can lead the smoker to a very serious illness as stated above. So we say cigarette is a refined tobacco with insecticide (nicotine) and toxic sheet of paper and a filter, which are all chemicals processed. Now when we smoke cigarette, this tobacco turns to carbon dioxide and carbon monoxide, and such as tars (carcinogenic). When carbon dioxide and carbon monoxide are combined, they produce FREE RADICALS (free electrons) as proven by scientist. Free radicals are electrons without atoms (very harassing and aggressive electrons). An electron and an atom when combined or put together produce ENERGY. The human body has already its atoms and its equivalent electrons which give us energy. Each puff of cigarette contains thirty-two (30-32) electrons (as proven by scientists) multiply by the number of puffs per stick of cigarette multiply by the number of sticks of cigarette we smoke per day. The electrons from the smoke admitted into the body struggle with the electrons already in the body and eat up the body atoms produced meant for the citizen electrons, why? because they are fresh and they are strong. These foreign electrons (free radicals) do not last for long, they last for twenty-four hours and within this period they cause terrible harm to the body. They are like Boko Haram (free radicals), this organization will die out in couple of years but it will cause terrible and horrible tragedy, if not stopped. So stop free radicals (the boko haram in your body) by stopping smoking. The remaining electrons which have no atoms must also live, they slowly attack the body cells. Any sickness can be a major illness after many years.

THE DEVIL OF CIGARETTE SMOKE

Illness mostly known are: 1. STROKE; 2. CANCER' 3. TUMOUR; 4. ULCER and so on. Carbon is an element which, when taken in excess make one feels tired always, leading to serious sickness. So we say carbon produce fatigue. So when free electrons are in excess they invade the heart to influence the brain and cause the following:

1. SELFISHNESS
2. GREEDINESS
3. JEALOUSY
4. CORRUPTION
5. HATRED

These are great enemies of the world. They are enemies fighting mankind to destroy them. We now know them so let us be cautious, and avoid them

NITROGEN = 14 atoms + 28 electrons or molecules (as published in news letter yrs ago)

CO_2 = 44 electrons + No atom (published in news letter yrs ago)

By these mathematics we can now be very careful with cigarette smoking. This smoke kill hundreds of people a day. It is as dangerous as the gun even terrible than the gun. The gun kill one at a time but the smoke kill hundreds at a time and the worse of it is, some of the victims suffer illness for many years before they are killed. If we can stop cigarette smoking, our cities will be wonderful cities to live. It's stressful and uncomfortable if non smoker has smokers around him smoking. Truth is only one and that's the truth, smokers are selfish and do not consider how other people feel when they are smoking around them, even when others are dying they only think of their satisfaction at that particular moment. The bible says in; 1Corinthians 3:16-17 "Do you not know that you are the temple of God and that the Spirit of God dwells in you? If anyone defiles the temple of God, God will destroy him. For the temple of God is holy, which temple you are." Again 1Corinthians 6:19 also says "Do you not know that your body is the temple of the Holy Spirit who is in you, whom you have from God, and you are not your own? For you are bought at a price; therefore glorify God in your body and in your spirit, which are God's." This is a plain sayings and you do not need explanation therefore why do people smoke. They are killing themselves and killing innocent people. The smoker and the sniper are no difference.

THE BIBLA COMPANION

ANOINTING:- Mark 5:22-23, 6:5-6, 13; 1Sam. 16:12-13, 9:16, 10:1; Exodus 30:22-30; Lev. 8:10-12; 1Kings 19:16, 1:39; 2Kings 9:1-7; James 5:13-15; Luke 9:1, 10:1; Mark 6:7; Hebr. 6:2-3; Acts 8:17, 13:3; 2Tim. 1:6; Deut. 34:9; 1Tim. 4:14;

ABORTION:- Gen. 38:7-11; Isaiah 66:7, 59:4; Job 15:35; Psalm 7:14

ANOINTING CLOTHES:- Acts 19:11-12, 6; Matt. 14:36; Mark 5:27-27; 2Kings 2:13-1-15

ANOINTING:- Acts 8:17-18,2-3;

ANGELS:- Gen. 16:9-11, 18:2-3, 19:1-2, 28:12; John 1:51; Luke 2:9-101, 1:11-13, 1:18-19,26,30; Matt. 2:13,18:10;Hebr. 1:14; Ex. 3:2; Gen. 31:24; Gen. 32:24,30;17:1 Matt. 1:20; 3:16; Gen. 18:12-16; John 5:4; Luke 1:19; Hebr. 1:6,7,13; Gen. 15:1

ANGELS OF THE SEVEN CHURCHES:- Rev. 2:1, 8,12,18; 3:1, 7, 14,

APPOINTMENT OF APOSTLES, PASTORS AND ELDER:- Luke 10:1, 9:1, 11:49, 3:13-19; Matt. 10:1-2;

1Tim. 2:7; 2Tim. 1:11; 1Cor. 12:28; Mark 3:13-19.

ANGELS:- Gen. 16:9-11, 18:2-3, 19:1-2, 28:12; John 1:51; Luke 2:9-101, 1:11-13, 1:18-19,26,30; Matt. 2:13,18:10;Hebr. 1:14; Ex. 3:2; Gen. 31:24; Gen. 32:24,30;17:1 Matt. 1:20; 3:16; Gen. 18:12-16; John 5:4; Luke 1:19; Hebr. 1:6,7,13; Gen. 15:1

ALMIGHTY GOD:- Deut. 32:39; Isaiah 43:10-11; 44:6; 45:5,18; Rev. 1:8, 11, 18; 22:13; 19:16; 4:8,11; 11:17; Zech. 14:9b; Deut. 6:4; 4:35,39; Ex. 33:20, 23; 1Timothy 6:16; Daniel 2:22; John 6:46; matt. 11:27. 1Cor. 8:6; Jer. 10:12-13; Jer. 32:17

ADULATERY:- Deut. 22:22-27; Gal. 5:19.

CITIZENSHIP IN HEAVEN:- Hebr. 9:28, 12:28, 11:16; Matt. 26:28; Eph. 2:12,19; Hebr. 11:16; Phil. 3:20-21; 2Cor. 5:1-3.

RAPTURE:- 1Thess. 4:13-17; 2Kings 2:11; Matt. 27:60-64; Acts 1:9-11; 1Cor. 15:5-8; Rev. 11:8-18, 4:7-11. 19:13-20, 16:15; 2Peter 3 -13.

RAINBOW:- Gen. 9:13-17.

RESURRECTION:- John 11:28-35, 5:28-35; Matt. 22:23-33, 27:52-53; 1Cor. 15:12-26; 1Thess.13:18; Matt. 27:52-53; Mark 16:6; Luke. 24:24-50; 1Peter 1:3; Phil. 3:10; Acts 24:15.

POWER OF PROPHECY:- Matt. 21:21; Ezek. 37:1-19; John 11:24-26; 2Kings 4:2-3; 1Kings 17:14-16

PRAYER:- Acts i2:5; 1:14,46,42; 10:2 Luke 24:53; Matt. 18:18-20; 17:21; 1Thess, 5:17-19; Eph. 6:18;Math. 26:41; Luke18:1; Phil. 1:4; Acts 12:5

QUALIFICATION FOR DIVORCE (bases for divorce);-1Cor. 7:15; Prov. 30:20; Mark 10:11-12; Matt. 19:9; Jer. 3:1; Deut. 24:1-4.

DIVORCE:- Deut. 24:14, Matt. 5:31-32,19:3-9; 1Cor. 7:10-16, 27-28,39; Mala. 2:16; Mark 10:3-12; Rom. 7:2-3; Jer. 3:1. Hebr. 2:16.

DESCRIMINATION:- Acts 10:34; Jam. 2:2-9; Rom. 2:11; Gal. 2:6; 1Tim. 5:21;Deut. 1:17, 10:17.

LAYING ON OF THE HANDS:- 1Tim. 4:14; Acts 8:17, 13:3; James 5:13-15; Hebr. 6:2; Mark 6:5-7; Rom. 10:17; 1Tim. 2:22.

BUILD AND LIVE IN:- Rom. 5:12-14; Acts 5:1-15; Isaiah65:17-25.

BLESSING:- Deut. 28:1-14; Rom. 4:7-8; Psalm 1:1-3; 3Jn. 2

BLOODSHED:- Gen. 9:6; Rev. 13:10; Nun. 35:33; Matt. 26:32; 2Sam. 16:7-8, 3:30.

HOLY GHOST:- Joel 2:28; Rom. 8:11-16, 26-279:1; Acts 10:38, 44-48; John 14:25-26, 16:7; 1Cor. 2:13, 14:2; Exo. 31:3; Acts 1:5, 8, 4:4-8, 2:1-4, 19:2-6, 13:9, 7:51. Luke 11:13, 3:22, 4:1, 12:12; 1John 5:6-7; Eph. 1:13, 4:30; 1Sam. 10:10; Matt. 1:20, 3:11, 12:31

MY POTENTIALS:- Eccl. 10:6-7; Jer. 18:1-4; Rom. 9:20-22; 1John 4:4,13; Psalm 68:1DEPRESSION Numb. 11:11-25; 1Kings 19:4

BOASTING:- Rom. 11:18, 12:3; Prov. 25:14, 27:1; Gal. 6:3

PROMISE;- Deut. 6:10-19, 7:12-16; Eccl. 10:7; Rom. 5:1; Psalm 116:14, 76:11; Jonah 2:9,1:16; Judges 11:30

JESUS PRAYED:- Luke 18:1, 11:1, 5:16, 9:18,29, 6:12; Mark 6:46, 14:32,35, 14:36; Matt. 14:23, 26:36,41, John 17; Acts 13:3

JESUS VANISHED:- Luke 24:31, 4:29-30; John 7:30, 10:39, 12:36,8:59

TRANSFER OF POWER:- 2Kings 2:9-15, (2Kings 5:19-27, 13:20-21); Matt. 16:19; John 20:22-23; Luke 9:1,10,10:1,17; Acts 13:3; Mark 6:7.

TEMPTATION:- Psalm 11:4-5, 95:8; Jam. 1:2-15; 1Cor. 10:13; 1Thess. 3:5; Matt. 26:4, 6:13; Job 1:8; Heb. 4:15; 2Peter. 2:9

DIVISION:- Ex. 8:22-23; 1Cor. 1:10; John 10:18-21, 7:43; 1Cor. 11:18, 3:3; Rom. 16:17-18; Acts 15:1.

GIVING:- Prov. 11:24; 2Cor. 9:6-10; Prov. 28:8,27, 3:9-10; Eccl. 11:1; Luke 6:38; Matt. 7:2; 1Kings 17:15-16; Gen. 22:16-17; Acts 20:35, 9:6-30-40; Phil. 4:14-15; Dan. 4:27; Psalm 30:9; 6:5; Prov, 19:17

CHILD TRAINING:- Prov. 28:13, 29:17, 6:20-24, 13:24, 3:11-12, 19:18, 22:6, 5:20-26, 22:6; Eph. 6:1-3; Gen. 18:19; Deut 6:7

ORDINATION OF PASTORS:- Exodus 29:7-9, 28:40; Num. 11:25; Mark 3:13-14; John 13:3-4; Acts 15:23;

HOMOSEXUALITY:- Lev. 18:22, 20:13; Rom. 1:24,26-27; Gen. 19:5-6; Deut. 22:5, 23:17; Judges 19:22-24; Mark 10:6-9.

IDLE WORDS:- Matt. 5:22, 12:35-37, 15:11,17-20; 1Peter 2:12, Psalms 34:13-14, 52:2; 2Tim. 2:16; Phil. 2:14-15. Luke 6:45; James 3:5-9; Eph. 4:29-31, 5:4; Romans 6:16; Colo. 3:8-9; 4:6; Lev. 24:14; Prov, 4:23

FAITH:-James 1:5-8; Matt. 7:7; Mark 11:22-24, 6:2; Hebr. 11:1, 3-6, 16-17; John 3:11-12; 3:18; Gal. 3:7-11; Gen. 1:1-4, 6,9,11,14,20; Rom. 10:14-17; Eph. 2:8-10; John 3:11-12, 18.

WOMEN TO KEEP SILENT IN CHURCH:- 1Cor. 14:34-37,33,40; 1Tim 2:11-15; Matt. 7:21-23; James 2:10-11; 1Tim. 5:20-21; 2Thess. 3:14-15; 1Tim. 5:2

WOMEN PASTOR:- Roman 16:1

WISDOM:- Prov. 4:5-7, 5:1-2, 14:33, 21:22,24:3-7; Isaiah 5:13; Hosea 4:6; Eze. 22:26; Matt. 13:44; Eccl. 9:13-18, 10:10

PROPHETESS:- Ex. 15:20; Judges 4:4; Luke 2:36; Neh, 6:14; Acts 21:8

FALSE PROPHETS:- Jer. 23:21, 25-26, 2:8; Deut. 18:20-22; Luke 8:10; Lev. 19:31,11; 1John 4:7; James 2:5; 1John 5:1-3, 4:16-21, 3:14-17; Luke 22:50-53, 6:27; 1John 3:10, 14, 17, 19-20; Mark 12:30-31.

LAZINESS:- Prov. 10:2, 13:11, 20:21, 21:5-6, 28:20; Hab. 2:6; Luke 12:19-20; Dan. 4:27; Eccl. 10:18

LOVE OF MOMEY:- Hebr. 13:5; James 5:18; 1Tim. 6:7-10; Luke 18:18-25

LIES:- Gen. 12:11-20, 20:2, 26:7, 27:5-34, 18:12-16; Joshua 2:1-15; 1Kings 13:1-31; Prov. 12:20,22, 13:3.

LIBATION:- Jer. 7:17-20, 19:13; Colo. 2:8.

LOVE:- Matt. 5:43-38; 1Cor. 13:1-13, 4:1; Prov. 10:12, 11:7; Acts 2:44-45; 1Sam. 18:1-4; Rom. 13:8-10; Gal. 5:13-14; Eph. 5:2; C0lo. 3:14; Lev.

19:18; Mark 12:31; 1Jn. 3:10-11; 1Jn. 4:7-12,16-20. Deut. 6:5; Psalm 31:23; Jn. 13:34-35, 15:13; Zech. 8:17. Rom. 12:9,5:8-10.

THE END:- Rev. 7:2-3, 9:1-12, 20:11-15; 1Peter 4:17-18; 2Peter 2:4-11; Matt. 24:3-7, 23-26,29-31,36-51

SUNDAY WORSHIP:- John 20:19, 26; Acts 20:7, 1Cor. 16:2-3; Ex. 12:16.

SMOKING:- Isaiah 55:2; Job 41:19-20; Hab. 2:13; Prov. 16:25; Acts 17:16-17; 1Cor. 3:16-17.

STEALING:- Lev. 19:11; Ex. 20:15; Deut. 5:19; Romans 13:9; Josh.7:20-21; Lev. 19:11.

STUDY:- 2Tim. 2:15, 3:7, 16; Rom. 15:4.1Tim. 4:6,13; Prov. 4:13; Acts 17:11; Psalm 119:105.

SABBATH:- Mark 2:27-28, 3:4; Lev. 26:2, 19:30,25:35-36, 23:15-16, 35-36; Ex. 12:16, 20:8,9-11.23:12; Gen. 2:2; Isaiah 58:13-14,56:2.

SPIRITUAL EYES:- Num. 22:31; Gen. 21:19; 2Kings 6:17; Luke 24:30-31.

EXPENSIVE SACRIFICE:- 2Kings 3:26-27; John 3:16-18; Rom. 5:8; 2Chro. 7:5; Judges 11:39-40

EATING OF BLOOD:- Gen. 9:4-5; 1Sam. 14:32-34; Lev. 17:14; Deut. 12:16, 23-25.

SALVATION:- Luke 19:10; Gen. 1:26; Gen. 3:1-4; Colo. 2:8-15; 2Cor. 5:21; Hebr. 7:22; Gal. 4:4-5; Ezek. 22:30; Isaiah 53:1-12, 1:18-20; Jer. 33:14-16; John 3:14-19,20-36,; Matt. 26:56, Eph. 3:9-12, 2:7-8,12-14; Isaiah 14:12-14; Rev. 12:7-11; Job 9:24; Luke 4:6; Matt. 28:18; Mark 16:16. Rom. 10:9-13, 12:1-2; 1Jn. 1:8-9; Jn. 20:31; Prov. 28:13.

SIN:- Gen. 31:19; Josh. 7:20-21; Gen. 38:13-16; Gen. 39:12-18; Rom. 1:22-32, 2:11-12; Isaiah 3:16-26; Mark 12:38-40; John 3:17-18, 27; 1Sam.

2:25; Hebr. 10:26, 31,23; James 2:10-11; 1Peter 3:12-16; Acts 5:1-11; Hosea 8:2-7; Matt. 11:12.

SON OF GOD:- Isa. 9:6; Dan. 3:25; Matt. 3:17; Jn. 1:18,5:19; Acts 8:37; Gal. 4:4; 2Peter 1:17; Heb. 5:8; Rom. 1:4,8:3,32; 1Jn. 5:10, 2:23-24.

SPIRITUAL EYES:- Num. 22:31; Gen. 21:19; 2Kings 6:17; Luke 24:30-31.

JUDGMENT OF THE UNGODLY:- 1Peter 4:17-19; Jude 6; 2Peter 2:4; 1Thess. 4:13-18; Zeph. 1:13-18; Mala. 4:1-3; Matt.:- 24:1:32; Isaiah 13:9-16.

TONGUES:- Joel 2:28; Acts 2:1-2, 10:44-48; Cor. 14:1-39; Eccl. 8:8

MARRIAGE BONDAGE:-(qualifications for divorce):- 1Cor. 7:10-16, 39; Rom. 7:2-3; Mark 10:11-12; Matt. 19:3-6; Prov. 30:20.

QUALITIES OF GOOD WIFE TO MARRY:- Prov. 12:4, 14:1, 31:10-31, 1cor. 11:7.

THE DAY OF THE LORD:- Matt. 24:36; Acts 1:7; 1Thess. 5:1; Deut. 29:29

TALENT:- Luke 19:11-27; Deut. 8:17-18, 9:3; Matt. 25:14-30.

TONGUES:- Joel 2:28; Acts 2:1-26, 19:4-6; 1Cor. 14:1-33; Eccl. 8:8.

MARRIAGE:- Colo. 3:18-19; Prov. 18:22, 9:13, 3:5, 19:14, 31:10, 27:2-3, 30:23, 5:18-23; Eph. 5:21-32; Gen. 2:24, 24:51-53; 1Peter. 3:2-7; Mark 12:20-25; Psalm 127:2-3; 1Cor. 7:34-39,1-16; Titus 2:2-5; 1Peter 3:1; Rev. 21:1-4; 1Tim. 3:11; Rom. 8:8-9, 26-28, 7:2-4; Matt. 5:31-32, 19:3-9, 22:23-32; Hebr. 13:4, 7:4-9;Exodus 22:16; Eccl. 4:8-12, 9:1; Jer. 29:6

FASTING AND PRAYER:- Acts 14:23, 9:9, 10:30, 13:23; Gal. 5:22; Matt. 4:2-4, 6:16-18; Gen. 126; Exodus 34:28-30; Daniel 101:1-3; Luke 2:37; Joel 2:12; Mark 9:29; Esther 4:3; Rom. 14:17; 1Cor. 7:5,8:8; Isa.58:3-16.

FINANCIAL BLESSING:- 3John 2; 2Cor. 8:9; Luke 6:36

FAMILIAR SPIRITS:- Exodus 22:18, 21:18; 2Kings23:10, 21:6, 23:24, 17:17; Lev. 19:31, 20:6, 27, 19:26, 21:27;Deut.18:10; Isaiah 8:19; 2Chron. 33:6; 1Sam. 28:7,9.

FORGIVENESS:- Matt. 18:21-22, 6:14-15, 18:23-35, 5:, 23-25,39-48,; Eph. 6:12; Gal. 6:7-10, 5:25-26; Lev. 19:17-18; Deut. 32:32-35; Hebr. 10:30-31; Luke 15:20; Rom. 5:10-12, 16:20; 2Cor. 2:10-11.

FORNICATION:- Deut. 22:28-29; Gal. 5:19

VIOLENCE TO WIVES:- 1Peter 3:7; Col. 3:19; Eph. 6:8-10; Mala. 2:16; Prov. 20:29; Gen. 2:18, 21-24

WATER BAPTISM:- John 3:5-27, 3:22-27, 6:44; Matt. 3:6, 11, 13-17,13-16, 28:19; Mark 1:8-10, 15, 16-18; Rom. 6:3-5, 10:9-10, 8:15-16; Acts 8:13, 38-39, 2:38, 41, 16:33,10:47-48, 18:8; 1Cor. 10:2; Colo.2:12; 1Peter 3:21; Luke 3:21; Eph. 2:4-9, 4:5; 1Cor.12;13; Hebr. 6:1-2;

DRUNKENNESS:- Gen. 9:20-24, 19:30-38; Isaiah 5:11-12,22; Prov. 31:2-6, 23:20-21, 29-32, 20:1, 21:17; Joel 1:5; Jer. 25:27,35:5-6; Gal. 5:21; Hab. 2:15-16; Eph. 5:18; Num. 6:13; 1Tim. 5:23; Lev. 10:9-10;Eze. 44:21

BATTLE BETWEEN CHRIST AND SATAN:- Luke 4:6; Matt. 28:18; John 14:30, 12:31

WHO ARE CHRISTIANS:- Gal. 3:26-29; Eph. 2:4-10; Acts 11:25; Luke 15:7-10; Mark 9:39; Matt. 7:21-25; Matt. 24:5, 23-26; Hebr. 11:6; Psalm 82:6; John 10:34-35.

COMMUNION:- Exodus 12:5-14; John 6:33-35,47-58; Luke 22:15-20; Matt. 26:26-30; 1Cor. 11:23-30, 5:7-11, 10:16-17; Acts 20:7; Mark 14:22-25.

THE CAUSE OF POVERTY:- Prov. 10:4; 12:24; 13:4,18; 15:27; 19:15,24,27, 20:4,13,22; 21:25; 22:7,8,13; 23:6-8; 26:13-16; 28:8,22; 1Tim. 6:17

VISION:- Acts 16:9-10, 10:10-11, 19-20, 18:9-10, 23:11; Daniel 10:2-8; Hab. 2:3; Prov. 29:18; 1Kings 3:5, 15; 2Cor. 12:14.

CHARITY:- 1Cor. 13:2-4, 141; Colo. 3:14; 2Tim. 2:22; 1Peter 4:8; 2Peter 1:7; 3John 6; Acts 16:25-35;

Prov. 21:13,29:13, 22:2,9, 28:27.

HOLY GHOST BAPTISM:- Acts 2:1-4; 10:44-47; 9:17-18; 19:2-7; Matt. 3:11, Rev. 2:10;

HATRED:- Gal. 5:20.

CHRIST AS A SURETY FOR CREATION OF MAN:- Hebrews 7:22; Genesis 1:26; Luke 19:10

TITHE:- Hebr. 7:8-9: Ex. 16:36; Num. 18:21-28; Gen. 14:20, 28:20-22; Neh. 10:35; Deut. 14:22-28, 8:18, 26:12-13; 1Cor. 16:1-2, 9:13-14; Matt. 22:21, Matt. 21:33-40, 23:23; Mala. 1:7-8, 3:8-10; Levit. 27:31-34; Prov. 3:9-10. 1Cor. 16:1-2, Job 38:4; 1Sam. 25:21; Matt. 23:17.

TITHE - PASTORS:- Numb. 18:26; Neh. 10:38; 1Chron. 9:26

PRIDE:- Prov. 13:10, 15:25, 16:5,18, 28:25

IDOLS:- Jer. 10:3-5,8-9,11; 50:38; Psalm 78:58, 115:4-10, 135:15-18; Ex. 32:2-14; 1John 5:21; Acts 15:20; Rev. 2:14; 1Cor. 8:4; Lev. 19:4;

IDOL WORSHIP:- 1Corinthians 8:4-5; Psalm 16:4;Psalm 14:1; Ez. 8:7-18; 23:35-39; Jer. 2:27; 50:38; Acts 14:11-16; 15:20; 17:23; Ex. 23:13,24; 20:5, 32:2-4; Deut. 4:15-20,23-24; 6:14-16, 27:15; Lev. 19:4; Rev. 2:14; 1John 5:21; Roman 1:23;

CURSE:- Jer. 11:3; Gal. 3:10; Deut. 27:15-26, 28:15-68, 21:23. Prov. 20:20; Prov. 3:33, 26:2; Eccl. 10:20, 5:4-9; Lam. 5:7; Deut. 27:15-26.

VOW:- Eccl. 5:4-7; Job. 22:27-28; Psalm 56:12; 66:13-14; Numb, 30:2; Judges 11:30-40; Gen. 28:20,

HEAVENLY AND EARTHLY DAYS:- 2Peter 3:8; Psalm 90:4

REFUGEE camps:- Num. 35:6,11-15; Joshua 20:6, 20:2,7-9, 21:13,21, 27,32,38.

RETIREMENT OF THE PRIESTS:- Numbers 8:24-26

RESURRECTION:- matt. 27:52-53, 22:23-33; Mark 16:6; Luke 24:34-50; Rev. 20:5; 1Pet. 1:3; Phil. 3:10; 1Cor15:12-21; John 11:24,26

RICHES AND BLESSINGS:- Prov. 10:6,22; 11:11,24; 19:4; 24:35; 20:21; 22:2,7,9; 28:13,25,27; Gen. 24:35, 26:12-14; Deut. 15:7,11; 1Tim. 6:18-19; Rom. 12:9-11.

SPIRITUAL WARFARE:- 2Cor. 10:3-6; Eph. 6:12-16; Josh. 5:13-15, 6:20, 7:24-26; Exo. 18:22; Josh. 6:20; Matt. 17:21, 12:43-45;Rev. 12:11; Matt. 12:43-45; Mark 3:14-15, 5:1-13, Rev. 12:7-11; Matt. 17:21

ENVY:- Mark 15:10; Matt. 27:18, 20:6-11; Prov. 23:17, 3:31; Psalm 73:3, 106:16; 1Sam. 18:9,29; Num. 12:1-3; Jam. 3:14; Esther 5:13; Rom. 13:13; Acts 17:5; Gal. 5:26. Num. 12:1-3; James 3:14; Esther 5:13; Roman 13:13; Acts 17:5; Gal. 5:26; 1Tim. 6:4.

0FFERING:-

Sin Offering:- Lev. 4:1-35

Peace Offering:- Lev. 3:1-17, 7:15

Burnt Offering:- Lev. 6:9-14, 9:23-24, 7:8

Wave Offering:- Lev. 10:14-15, 22:14, 7:30,34; Num. 18:11.

THE TWELVE PLAGUES:- Exo. 7:10-12, 7:20,8:6, 8:16, 8:24, 9:6, 9:9, 9:26, 10:5, 10:21, 11:4, 14:21-30.

BRIBERY:- Deut. 27:25; Ez. 22:12; Prov. 17:23, 15:27, 21:13; 1Sam. 8:2-5, 12:3; Ex. 23:8; Acts 24:24-27; Isa. 5:23, 1:23; Luke 3:12-14; Num. 35:31

ABORTION:- Isa. 66:7-9, 59:7; Job 15:35; Rom. 3:15; Prov. 1:16, 6:17.

POLYGAMY:- Gen. 16:3, 29:30, 28:9; 1Sam. 30:5; 1Kings 11:1-3.

TAKING BACK MY BIRTHRIGHT:- Rom. 9:10-13;Gen. 25:21-34, 27:21-38; Prov. 16:25, 24:4; 1Chro. 17:15.

CHANGING YOUR DESTINY BY PROPHETIC DIRECTION:- Heb. 12:16-17; Gen. 25:22-23, 30-34;Prov. 23:4.

PUNISHMENT OF REBELLION:- Deut.32:16-30,35;Psalm.78:56;Rom.10:19;Jer.50:31-38,51:6-7,24,26,51

REINCARNATION:- Matt. 17:10-13; Mark 9:11-13.

SECURITY OF ANCESTRAL PROPERTY:- Prov. 5:7-11; Gen. 20:12-14, 24:2-8, 28:1-4.

APOSTLE PAUL'S SUFFERINGS:- 2Cor. 11:24-25; Acts 16:22-24, 21:30-33, 14:19-20, 23:12-13.

MIRACLES OF APOSTLE PAUL:- Acts 14:3, 14:8-12, 16:25-26, 19:11-16, 2-7, 20:19-20, 28:3-6.

THE SEVEN TENENTS OF JESUS CHRIST

1. **The prophecies about Jesus:** a. Isaiah 9:6 b. Isaiah 53:2-12 c. Isaiah 7:14 d. Luke 1:30-35 e. Deut. 18:18-19; f. John 5:46
2. **The birth of Jesus Christ:** a. Luke 2:6-7 b. Luke 2:9-14
3. **The Ministry of Jesus Christ:** a. Mark 1:9-11 b. Mark 1:14-20 c. Matt. 3:21-23 d. Luke 4:18-19
4. **The Crucifixion of Jesus Christ:** a. Mark 15:21-23 b. Mark 15:33-39 c. Exo. 26:31-33 d. Luke 23:33-38,46,53 e. John 19:30
5. **The burial of Jesus Christ:** John 20:38-42; Isaiah 53:9; Luke 23:5; Matt. 27:59-60; Mark 15:45-46.
6. **The resurrection of Jesus Christ:** a. John 20:11-20 b. Luke 24: 6-9, 18-35 c. John 20:24-31
7. **Ascent ion of Jesus Christ:-** Mark 16:19; Luke 24:51; Acts 1:2, 9-.11
8. **Deity of Jesus Christ:-** Acts 2:33; Heb. 1:13, 10:12; Matt. 12:32; Psalm 110:1(Mark 12:36); John 17:5, 16:28.

Jesus Christ was made an accurse of God: Deut. 21:23; Galatians 3:13.

THE SEVEN DEADLY SINS:-

LUST:- 1John 2:16; Gen. 3:6; Eccl. 5:10

GLUTTONY:- Matt. 11:19; Luke 7:33-35; Deut. 21:20-21; Rom. 12:2; Isaiah 5:11; James 2:14-24; Prov. 23:21; Gal. 5:16-26.

GREED:- Luke 16:4, 12:15; Prov. 15:27; Matt. 5:39-40;

SLOTH:- Prov. 26:13-16, 19:24, 15:19, 13:4;Phil. 4:13; Colo. 4:1-7, 3:23; 2Thess. 3:10; Prov. 12:24

WRATH:- Rev. 14:8; James 1:20; 1Tim. 2:8, Heb. 10:30.

ENVY:- Prov. 28:22; Mark 15:10; Matt. 27:18; Job 5:2

PRIDE:- Prov. 8:13, 3:7, 16:5, 15:25; 16:18; 1John 2:16

What You Can Do With The Psalms

1. Psalm 1. .... Prevent harmful association, Drugs and Alcohol.
2. Psalm 2. .... Conquer Enemies, Protection in Travelling and vehicle.
3. Psalm 3. .... Relief of Tension, Headaches, Backaches and Fear.
4. Psalm 4. .... Sleep Well and Win any court case. alleviate insomnia.
5. Psalm 5. .... Spiritual Growth and Special Blessings.
6. Psalm 6. .... Cure Eye diseases, Repentance.
7. Psalm 7. .... Gain Victory in court/justice ruling and to Uncross Yourself.
8. Psalm 8. .... Increase Business and Gain Confidence.
9. Psalm 9. .... Cure Male Children. overcome evil forces
10. Psalm 10. .... Defeat Evil Spirit and Strength to Persevere.
11. Psalm 11. .... To Bring Back a departed Husband or Wife. And Overcome Fear.
12. Psalm 12. .... Overcome destruction Gossiping, Silence Rumor Mongers and Anxiety.
13. Psalm 13 .... Protection From Unnatural Death and Bodily Harm (depression).
14. Psalm 14 .... Against Misfortune, Slander and Mistrust.
15. Psalm 15 .... Remove Evil Spirits and cast away resentments (depression).
16. Psalm 16 .... Change sorrow to joy, Find the name of a thief.
17. Psalm 17 .... Safety throughout the Day and For Eternal Life. Make Enemy divert from Evil.
18. Psalm 18 .... Recovery from Illness, Protect Your Home, Prevent an Attack.
19. Psalm 19 .... For God's Love and Direction, Faith in God and His Blessing. Remove Illness.

20. Psalm 20 .... For favorable Court Judgment, Return a Lover, prevail over Suffering.
21. Psalm 21 .... For Abundant Spiritual Blessing, Have Favor From Authority.
22. Psalm 22 .... For Safety in Travelling. To be Saved From Discouragement.
23. Psalm 23 .... For Pure and Peace of Mind, Divine Wisdom, vision.
24. Psalm 24 .... To Avoid immoral Temptations, To Deal With Difficult Times.
25. Psalm 25 .... For Divine Enlightenment, Forgive Others, Receive Spiritual Direction.
26. Psalm 26 .... To Have Financial Success, Prevent Imprisonment, Obtain Confidence.
27. Psalm 27 .... To Be Kindly Welcomed, To Unite Family.
28. Psalm 28 .... Appease with Enemy, Travelling Safety. Enemy Disarmament (stop).
29. Psalm 29 .... Cast out demons. Win in Game, Breakthrough in School, gain a friend back.
30. Psalm 30 .... For Good Health in times of sickness, To ask for Patience.
31. Psalm 31 .... To avoid Disgrace, To prevent Distress.
32. Psalm 32 .... To receive Grace, Love and Mercy.
33. Psalm 33 .... Fearful Attitude, Whenever One feel unloved.
34. Psalm 34 .... To Have Favor of Those in Authority, To Suppress arrogance.
35. Psalm 35 .... To Win In Any Court Case, Divine Help When Falsely Accused, Financial Help.
36. Psalm 36 .... To Stop Gossipers, Mental Improvement, Divine Wisdom.
       Conquer Envy.
37. Psalm 37 .... To Disable Enemy, To Stop People From Making You Escape Goat, Relax Nerves.
38. Psalm 38 .... To do away with Lust, Drive Away Evil and Evil Spirits From Your Home.

39. Psalm 39 .... Stress Relieve, Stand Alone Spirit.
40. Psalm 40 .... Strengthen Faith, Spiritual Assistance Over Frustration., Stop Evil Spirits
41. Psalm 41 .... Remove Depression, Cancel Bad Credit, Prevent Betrayal.
42. Psalm 42 .... Prophetic Gifts, Heal The Body, See things through Dreams.***
43. Psalm 43 .... To Be Delivered From Injustice.
44. Psalm 44 .... Protection From Assault, For Peace Among Marriage Couples.
45. Psalm 45 .... To Increase Speech Ability. *
46. Psalm 46 .... To Settle Quarrels, To Lift Ones Spiritual Strength. Peaceful Family.
47. Psalm 47 .... Pleasure, Joy, Happiness And Love in Marriage. Prov. 31:10-12
48. Psalm 48 .... For Hope When Despair.
49. Psalm 49 .... Increase Prophetic Ability, *** To Heal A Sick Person.***
50. Psalm 50 .... For Spiritual Eyes, To Get Out Of Trouble.
51. Psalm 51 .... Liberate from Guilty Conscience.
52. Psalm 52 .... Reject to Suffer Injustice, Divine Help.***
53. Psalm 53 .... For The Love Of God In Ones Heart.
54. Psalm 54 .... To See other's negative thoughts, Revenge Against Enemies.
55. Psalm 55,,,,,,,,,,,,,. Create Confusion Within Enemies, Overcome Fear Of Death.
56. Psalm 56 .... Return Wicked Plots to Sender. To Remove Evil Lust.
57. Psalm 57 .... For God's Mercy, Remove Love.
58. Psalm 58 .... Stop False Accusation, Suppress Liars.
59. Psalm 59 .... Eliminate Temptation, Destroy the power of Enemies.
60. Psalm 60 .... Do away with the past, Protection against Injury.
61. Psalm 61 .... Help For New House, Confrontation With the Law.

62. Psalm 62 .... Exchange Ones Luck, Divine Blessing, Fortify Spiritual Gifts.
63. Psalm 63 .... Self Encouragement, Make You Debtor pay you what they owe you.
64. Psalm 64 .... Remove Doubts, Prevent Accidents, Influence Over a Person.
65. Psalm 65 .... Be Lucky In All Ones Affairs. Thanks To God.
66. Psalm 66 .... Appreciation For Answered Prayer. For Luck in Game of Chance.
67. Psalm 67 .... Attract Friends, Strengthen marriage. Remove Frustration.
68. Psalm 68 .... Cast out Evil Spirit From a person, Receive Favorable Judgment.
69. Psalm 69 .... Liberate A person From Jail. Conquer Evil Habits. Curse Deliverance.
70. Psalm 70 .... Peace in the House, Drive Away people with wicked thoughts.
71. Psalm 71 .... Deliverance from Mental Instability. Strong Hope in God's Blessing.
72. Psalm 72 .... To Win The game of chance, Improve Finances, Attract Customers.***
73. Psalm 73 .... Eliminate Anger and resentment, For Money.**
74. Psalm 74 .... For Forgiveness of Sin, Attract Good Fortune, When Enemies After You.
75. Psalm 75 .... Job Promotion, Misunderstanding Between Friends, Forgiveness of offences.
76. Psalm 76 .... For chance to win a contest or games, When Encounter Dangerous Situation
77. Psalm 77 .... To Humble a proud Person, Restore Faith.
78. Psalm 78 .... For More Prophetic Power.***
79. Psalm 79 .... Do away with Opponent, Retaliate Wrong, Cause Downfall of Enemies.
80. Psalm 80 .... Protect Yourself Against An Error, To Shame Those Who Seek Your Downfall.

81. Psalm 81 .... Protect Yourself Against Sin,*** Maintain Godly Faith.
82. Psalm 82 .... To Obtain A Loan Easy and Quick From Bank or Someone.
83. Psalm 83 .... Return Evil To Sender.
84. Psalm 84 .... For a Prosperous Future.***
85. Psalm 85 .... Reconciliation with God, Cleansing of Transgression.
86. Psalm 86 .... For Victory (court, exams, School, Boxing, Soccer, etc.).
87. Psalm 87 .... To Become Prominent (games, movies, music, etc.).***
88. Psalm 88 .... For success in Job Interviews, renew friendship with a lover.
89. Psalm 89 .... For Healing (put your hand on the pain and pray this Psalm).
90. Psalm 90 .... Obtain high mark in Exam. Overcome Depression.***
91. Psalm 91 .... Protection against Evil and temptations.
92. Psalm 92 .... Appreciation and Gratitude for what the Lord has done for you.
93. Psalm 93 .... When one is in trouble with the Law and to comfort.
94. Psalm 94 .... Defeat Enemy and for justice to prevail.
95. Psalm 95 .... To see into the future and ability to predict, voice to worship.**
96. Psalm 96 .... To dream of numbers, To be strong spiritually.
97. Psalm 97 .... A Happy Family and A Happy Home.
98. Psalm 98 .... Peace Between Families and Family Members.
99. Psalm 99 .... Soul Purification, also This will bring Justice In All legal Proceedings.
100. Psalm 100 ... For strong general protection.
101. Psalm 101 ... Protection Against Demons. Break unhealthy and harmful habits.

102. Psalm 102 ...Fertility to be productive, To be physically strong and healed.**

103. Psalm 103 ...For God's Mercy. Forgiveness of Sins.**

104. Psalm 104 ...For Deliverance of Curse from our fathers.***

105. Psalm 105 ...To vanquish Bitterness, and to forget the past memories. Avoid someone.

106. Psalm 106 ...Faith in God and anointing: His power, His mercy and justice.

107. Psalm 107 ...To stop drunkenness.

108. Psalm 108 ...To be successful in Business***

109. Psalm 109 ...Return Evil To Sender.

110. Psalm 110 ...To subdue Enemy.

111. Psalm 111 ... To find a job of ones heart, For a new lover.

112. Psalm 112 ... For wisdom to study and supersede opponent, also enlarge ones territory.

113. Psalm 113 ... Pray this Psalm for a prosperous year. To obtain honor and popularity.

114. Psalm 114 ... If you want to dominate an institution or someone, then pray this psalm.

115. Psalm 115 ... For Business expansion. Also for a Clare mind and strong Faith.

116. Psalm 116 ... Give thanks to God for recovering from deadly illness or a breakthrough.

117. Psalm 117 ... After getting out of Depression or failure.

118. Psalm 118 ... To destroy the works of Satanic Forces. Give thanks to God.

119. Psalm 119 .. ALEPH 1-8 ... To be able to keep vow.

120. Psalm 119 .. BETH 9-16 ... To cleanse the heart and mind.

121. Psalm 119 .. GIMEL 17-24 ... Attract money. Improve one's finances.

122. Psalm 119 ...DALETH 25-32 ... For more Wisdom to learn.

123. Psalm 119 ... HE 33-40 ... Eliminate bad habits, and to have good habits.

124. Psalm 119 ... VAU 41-48 ... Make people do what you say.

125. Psalm 119 ... ZAIN 49-56 ... Helps one avoid sinning.

126. Psalm 119 ... CHETH 57-64 ... Maintaining Hope and not give in.
127. Psalm 119 ... TETH 65-72 ... Pray this to avoid confusion, Stress, and anxiety.
128. Psalm 119 ... JOD 73-80 ... For God's help to find a job.
129. Psalm 119 ... CAPH 81-88 ... To be delivered from persecution.
130. Psalm 119 ... LAMED 89-96 ... Pray this psalm to have mercy for other people.
131. Psalm 119 ... MEM 97-104 ... To Expand your Wisdom.***
132. Psalm 119 ... NUN 105-112 ... To have more Understanding.***
133. Psalm 119 ... SAMECH 113-120 ... Revitalize Hope
134. Psalm 119 ... AIN 121-128 ... For more profit out of one's own hard work.
135. Psalm 119 ... PE 129-136 ... Pray this psalm for sincerity humility and Clare mind.
136. Psalm 119 ... TZADDI 137-144 ... To avoid being under Tension (Stress).
137. Psalm 119 ... KOPH 145-152 ... Pray this to take away confusion.
138. Psalm 119 ... RESH 153-160 ... Coupled with your medication and med. Advice your health will be restored. This is for very ill person.
139. Psalm 119 ... SCHIN 161-168 ... Praises to God after breakthroughs.
140. Psalm 119 ... TAU 170-176 ... To ask for forgiveness of Sins***
141. Psalm 120 .... Disable Evil Tongues.
142. Psalm 121 ... For travelling Protection.
143. Psalm 122 ... To be able to deliver a better public speech. Also to prosper in business.
   For peace and security of the Church (peace to a troubled congregation).
144. Psalm 123 ... Help to find a job. To have more Fame. And favor from anybody.
145. Psalm 124 ... Overcome addiction and temptations.
146. Psalm 125 ... For a Healthy mind or brain. Also a study mind.
147. Psalm 126 ... Change from anguish to joy.

148. Psalm 127 … To discourage cheating. This psalm will make your children healthy.
149. Psalm 128 … For a happy and healthy home.
150. Psalm 129 … To destroy the power of oppression.
151. Psalm 130 … Control others and compel them to follow you.
152. Psalm 131 … To remove pride from one's life.
153. Psalm 132 … To be wealthy and enforce principle.
154. Psalm 133 … For strong friendship. To improve family tides.
155. Psalm 134 … Give you more desire for the word of God and be spiritual.
156. Psalm 135 … To receive reasonable portion of inheritance. Also to have good character.
157. Psalm 136 … To have a good presentation, negotiation and contract to your advantage.
158. Psalm 137 … To do away with envy and refuse evil.
159. Psalm 138 … To be spiritually bold.
160. Psalm 139 … To banish spiritual attacks. Insist to implement God's direction.
161. Psalm 140 … Make your ambition come true.
162. Psalm 141 … Pray this for more courage. And condemn lying tongues.
163. Psalm 142 … Reverse temptation. If you want to have answer to prayer.
164. Psalm 143 … To build up hope. For recovery from downfall.
165. Psalm 144 … Get rid of evil writings in life.
166. Psalm 145 … To win back slandered believers.
167. Psalm 146 … To do away with excessive confidence. And to have bread always.
168. Psalm 147 … Peace of mind and calm conscience.
169. Psalm 148 … Remove solitary, And Praising God.
170. Psalm 149 … Praise God always for being alive.
171. Psalm 150 … Daily morning worship to the Father Almighty.**

Psalms are powerful prayers which can be apply to achieve anything in life. But you need the instruction and direction to make it function to your amazement.

QUESTION AND ANSWERS

1. Gen. 11:26 What was the name of Abram's father?
2. Gen. 11:27How many sons had TERAH? Name them.
3. Gen. 11:27 Haran had how many children? Name them.
4. Gen. 11:29Who was Abram's wife?
5. In Genesis 11:31 Where did Terah the father of Abram intend to go, when he took Abram his son, Lot his grandson and Sarai his daughter-in-law?
6. Gen. 11:31 Where did Terah live with Abram, Lot and Sarai before he intended to move to CANAAN?
7. Gen. 12:1 What instruction did God give to Abram after his father was dead?
8. Gen. 12:13 Abram said to his wife Sarai to say to the Egyptians that he is his brother. Why did he say that?
9. Gen. 12:15,16 How was Abram blessed?
10. Gen. 12:10 Why did the King treated Abram that way?
11. Gen. 13:2 Abram's prosperity depended on what?
12. Gen. 13:7 What happened between the herdsmen of Abram and Lot?
13. Gen. 13:8 What did Abram say to Lot his brother?
14. Gen. 1310, Where did Abram go to dwell and Lot also pitch his tent.
15. Gen. 14:14 What did Abram do when he heard that his brother lot has been taken captive?
16. Gen. 14:18 What did Melchizedek do when Abram went and brought back his brother Lot and the sodonian captives and their goods?

1. Ans. Terah
2. Ans. Three sons. Abram, Nahor, Haran.
3. Ans. (a) Three, (b)Gen, 11:27 lot, Gen.11:29 Milchah, and Iscah
4. Ans. Sarai
5. Ans. He intended to go to CANAAN Gen. 10:19

6. Ans. He lived in Ur of the Chaldeans Acts 7:4

7. Ans. To get out of his family, and his father's house, to a land the Lord will show him. Gen. 11:9, Acts 7:2,3.

8. Ans. Because he was afraid the Egyptians will kill him because of her beauty Gen.12:13,14.

9. Ans. King Pharaoh treated Abram well for the sake of Sarai. He had sheep, oxen, male and female donkeys, male and female servants and camels.

10. Ans. Because he was interested in sarai not knowing she was Abram's wife and also there was famine and wanted to please Abram and because the Lord had to fulfill his promise. Gen. 12:10, Gen. 26:1, Gen. 12:15.

11. Ans. Livestock, Silver, Gold. Gen. 24:35, Gen. 26:14.

12. Ans. There was strife between them. Gen. 13:7

13. Ans. We are brothers do not let us strife between ourselves. 2Cor. 8:7, 1Cor. 8:7

14. Ans. Abram the part of Jordan called Canaan, and Lot the part of Jordan called Sodon near Gomorrah close to Zoar in Egypt. Gen. 13:10,1

15. Ans. Gen. 19:29.he gathered his army and went against them and overcame them

16. Ans. He blessed Abram. Hebr.7:1-10.

CREATION AND THE ORIGIN OF SIN

1. Who formed man? Ans. God. Gen. 1:26-27; Eph. 4:24
2. By what means God created man? Ans. Out of the dust of the ground. Job 33:4
3. Can any place conceals us from the sight of God? Ans. No . Jer. 23:23-24, Psalm 139:7
4. What is it, that makes us fear to meet God? Ans. Sin. Rom. 3:23, 2Cor.5:21, Rom. 6:16
5. What do we have to do when we sin?
   Ans. 1John 1:8-10, Confess and be truly sorry for our sins. Ask for a pardon and repent.
6. Adam and Eve had two sons. What are their names? Ans. Cain and Abel. Gen. 4:1-2.
7. Which of the two is older? (b) What is the meaning of Cain?
   Ans. Cain. (b) Acquired; Obtained; Got. Gen. 4:1.
8. What was Cain's profession? Ans. Tiller of the ground (farmer) Gen. 4:2
9. What was the profession of Abel? Ans. Keeper of sheep (shepherd). Gen. 4:2
10. What made Cain angry? Ans. Because his offering was rejected. Gen. 4:4-5
11. What did God tell Cain? Ans. To change his plan against Abel. Gen. 4:8
12. What did Cain do to Abel?
    Ans. He device evil device against Abel and killed him. Jer. 18:18, Gen. 4:8, Gen. 9:6.

SALVATION

1. Give four other names which has the same interpretation as salvation.

   a) redemption b) regeneration or mystery c) rescue d) born again

2. Can we by our own strength become the followers of Jesus Christ?

John 6:44 no one can came to me except the father which hath Sent me draw him, and I will raise him up at the Last day

3. What is salvation? Salvation is the saving of a person from sin or spiritual death. It is something that rescues Person from danger or total perish.

4a. Salvation is a free gift which every human being must receive, It leads to an everlasting life and redeems one from destruction. But this salvation is only found in the name of Jesus Christ.

   a] True b] False

4b. Give a quotation which confirms that salvation is found only in the name of Jesus.

Acts 4:12. neither is there salvation in any other: for there is none other name under heaven given among men whereby we must be saved

5. For all have sinned and fall short of the glory of God.

Quote the chapter in the bible which confirms this verse. Genesis 3.

6. Therefore if any man be in Christ he is a new creature, old things are passed away, all things are new.

This quotation is from 2Cor, 5:17. a] True b] False

7. What is the purpose of salvation? The purpose is to return all mankind (back) to God

8. Give a quotation in the bible which confirms that all mankind was on the verge of Lost.

1 Peter 2:25 For ye were as sheep going astray: but are now returned unto the shepherd and bishop of your souls.

RESTORATION OF SALVATION

2Cor. 5:21. For he hath made him to be sin: that we might be made the righteousness of God in him.

Q1. Who was made sin? --- Ans. Jesus

Q2. Who made him sin? --- Ans. The Father.

Q3. Why was he made sin? --- Ans. That we might be made the righteousness of God in Jesus Christ.

1Cor.1:21. For after that in the wisdom of God the world by wisdom knew not God, it pleased God

by the foolishness of preaching to save them that believe.

Q1. Which people were saved by the foolishness of preaching?

Ans. those who believed what was preached.

Q2. Why the bible said the foolishness of preaching.

Ans. 1Cor. 1:18

Ephesians 2:8-9. For by grace are ye saved through faith; and that not of yourselves: it is the gift of God. Not of works lest any man should boast.

Q1. By what means are we saved? --- Ans. Grace through faith.

Q2. Don't you think we are saved by ourselves because we had to give up ourselves

Ans. No, it is the grace of God through Jesus Christ.

BENEFIT OF SALVATION

Mark 13:10. And the gospel must first be published among all nations.

Q1. Why should the gospel first be published among all nations?

Ans. Because it is the right of all humans to be saved.

Mark 16:17-18 And these signs shall follow them that believe; In my name shall they cast out devils; they shall speak with new tongues; They shall take up serpents; and if they drink any deadly thing, it shall not hurt them; they shall lay hands on the sick and they shall recover

Q1. What signs did Jesus says shall follow them that believe in Him?

Ans. Casting out of devils, speaking in tongues, drink deadly things and not be hurt, take up serpents, and lay hands on the sick and they will recover.

Q2. Why speaking with new tongues, important?

Ans. It's a commandment from Jesus, It's a language given to believers to communicate with God, because if humans cannot understand this language then the devil also cannot Understand it. Only the one who gives this language understands it.

Q3. Why Jesus promise believers with casting out of demons?

Ans. Because Jesus did it and promised believers to do this to edify the church to glorify God.

Q4. Does that means the person in whom the demons are cast out is a devil or a witch or wizard?

Ans. No. The person is being possessed and tormented.

Discussion:

Psalm 51:12-13. Restore unto me the joy of thy salvation and uphold me with thy free spirit. Then I will teach transgressors thy way and sinners be converted unto thee.

Romans 8:1 There is therefore now no condemnation to them which are in Christ Jesus who walk not after the flesh, but after the Spirit.

8:31 What shall we say to these things? If God be for us, who can be against us?

8:32 He that spared not his own son, but delivered him up for us all, how shall he not with him also freely give us all things.

8:37 In all these things we are more than conquerors through him that love us.

ABOUT THE AUTHOR

I was born in the twin city of Sekondi-Takoradi in Ghana, to a Muslim father and a Christian mother. My father's family will not allow him to marry a woman of different faith, so out of love for him she converted to Islam. Several years into the marriage and seven children, my mother went back to Christ. Her decision did not sit well with my father, so they parted ways.

I worked as a payroll clerk at the State Construction Corporation in Takoradi, after graduating from Ahantaman Secondary School at Takoradi. My dream was to be an engineer seafarer, so I sought a degree in Internal Combustion Engines at Takoradi Polytechnic. A month after graduation, I was hired as Engine Cadet internship with a shipping company called Black Star Line (BSL).

During the course of my internship with BSL, news of the largest fishing company in West Africa, Mankoadze Fisheries, was offering full scholarships to recent Engine Cadets who were willing to attend Ghana Nautical College, I was sellected, then after graduation work for them. I graduated as a Second Engineer, and begun working for Mankoadze.

In 1977 a friend of mine introduced me to Buddhism, at the time it made a lot of sense to me so I converted. With the title of Acting Chief Engineer at Mankoadze, an opportunity to work for a state own construction company in Libya as Preventive Maintenance Engineer was presented to me in Ghana. I accepted, and worked in Libya for two years then moved to Italy with my family.

While in Italy I was still practicing Buddhism, and I thought of Christianity as the religion for losers. As a matter of fact, some Christian friends of mine invited me to their respective churches, but I turned them down. I had the notion that I knew it all, and that Christ could not do nothing for me. One morning in 1996, my wife told me had she had dream that Jesus was standing by our entrance door. I brushed her off then went about my business. Two weeks after, my wife and I heard my youngest son screening, we rushed to his room he told us he saw Jesus. I could not understand why was He doing this.

That Sunday my wife and my kids decided to go to church for the first time. Funny enough I dropped them off, but did not enter inside the church. That night I also had a dream where I saw the Throne of the Lord with multitude of angels worshiping the Lord. I continued to drop off my family every Sunday. This went on for about a month, until one Sunday I found myself standing in front of the church congregation accepting Christ as my lord and personal savior.

I became a committed member of the church, and through my commitment the Lord elevated me to the eldership roll, then years later I was ordained as a pastor. In the year 2000 I was transferred to the USA to replant the Bronx assemble. While doing so, I obtained my bachelor's degree in Theology from the Southern University College of Theology.

When I became a Christian I devoted myself to reading the Bible and understanding the message is giving to Christians. I noticed that many people including some Christian have abandoned their godly responsibility. I began to pray to the God for three years, and the Lord inspired me to write this book, "THE SAVING HERITAGE" for awareness.